P9-CNH-289

Better Than
MONEY

Build Your Fortune Using Stock Options and Other Equity Incentives—in Up *and* Down Markets

By David E. Gumpert

Copyright © David E. Gumpert, 2000

Published by Lauson Publishing Co.

P.O. Box 36

Needham, MA

Better Than
MONEY

Build Your Fortune Using Stock Options and Other
Equity Incentives—in Up *and* Down Markets

By David E. Gumpert

Copyright © David E. Gumpert, 2000

Published by Lauson Publishing Co.,

P.O. Box 36

Needham, MA 02494

All Rights Reserved

Printed in the United States of America

ISBN 0-9701181-2-0

No part of this book may be reproduced or transmitted in any form or by any means, graphic, electronic, or mechanical, including photocopying, recording, taping, or by any information storage or retrieval system without the permission in writing from the publisher.

This publication is sold with the understanding that the publisher is not engaged in rendering legal, accounting, or other professional service. Readers requiring legal advice or other expert assistance should seek out the services of a competent professional.

About the Author

David E. Gumpert is a successful entrepreneur and business author who has handed out and received stock options, and is now sharing his real-world lessons. As an entrepreneur, he cofounded NetMarquee Inc., an online direct marketing agency recently acquired by Circle.com (NASDAQ: CIRC). As NetMarquee's president and chairman, he helped formulate the company's stock option program, which led to all employees sharing in the proceeds from the company's sale. He is also president of Gumpert Communications Inc., a public relations agency based in Needham, MA.

Mr. Gumpert is a best-selling author of six books on small business, entrepreneurship, and marketing communications, including *How to __Really__ Create a Successful Business Plan*, *How to __Really__ Start Your Own Business,* and *How to __Really__ Create a Successful Marketing Plan*. One of his first books, *Business Plans that Win $$$* (coauthored with Stanley Rich), remains a classic more than 15 years after its original publication. He is also an experienced journalist, having served as a senior editor of *Inc.* magazine, an associate editor of *The Harvard Business Review,* and a staff reporter with *The Wall Street Journal.*

For my uncle, Ernst Gumpert, who
taught me so much that is truly important.

Table of Contents

Acknowledgements

I've written or coauthored six books, but this, my seventh, was probably the most involved because the subject of equity compensation is so complex. Fortunately for you, the reader, I had lots of help in making sure the book is useful and accurate.

Three individuals with deep expertise in equity compensation and entrepreneurship reviewed my original manuscript and provided important input, including suggestions and corrections that improved the book immensely.

Gabor Garai, a Boston lawyer who specializes in all matters associated with compensating executives in small-and-mid-size businesses and valuing companies, and is a partner with Epstein Becker & Green, a national firm, helped clarify a number of key issues.

Julian Lange, an assistant professor of entre-preneurship at Babson College in Wellesley, MA, made sure I expanded on points designed to improve the book's usefulness to job hunters.

And Joe Caruso, a consultant who works with dozens of emerging companies to help them in equity compensation and assorted other growth-related issues, provided important suggestions on the book's tone and overall strategy guidelines.

In addition to these three experts, the book benefited from the direct involvement of several professionals at my public relations agency, Gumpert Communications Inc. in Needham, MA. Dawn Ringel did much tedious copy editing. Rick Freedman developed the glossary and Internet resources. Sherry Alpert helped write chapter summaries and created the index. Patti Kane put her marketing, production, and layout skills to work in making sure the book was easy to follow and to read. Carla Bertonazzi dealt with many of the infinite production and publicity details that helped keep everyone on track. And a design consultant, Sybil Norwood, developed the book's cover.

And of course, I must thank my family. My son, Jason, provided important input from the viewpoint of a recent college graduate who just went through his initial job search. My daughter, Laura, a college student, was a sounding board on a number of concepts. And my wife, Jean, was her usual patient and forgiving self as I spent more evenings and weekends working on this book than I should have.

Introduction

The New American Lottery

Y ou're a 32-year-old graphic designer and you've just been offered a job at three-month-old Superfastgrowth.com—at a $5,000 cut in pay from your current job. You hate to take the pay cut because you can barely cover your personal expenses with your existing pay, but the new job comes with options to acquire 20,000 shares of stock in Superfastgrowth.com at ten cents a share. If Superfastgrowth.com ever goes public or is acquired, those shares could be worth enough that you could buy that condo you've been eying.

■ You're a 20-something just getting out of Harvard Business School and you've been doing the rounds of interviews with investment banking and consulting firms, a few of which have already offered jobs with annual salaries in excess of $100,000. But Superfastgrowth.com has just offered you the position of chief financial officer. The job pays less than half of what the other offers provide, but it comes with options to acquire 50,000 shares of Superfastgrowth.com at ten cents a share.

■ You're a carpenter and you've just provided an estimate of $30,000 to upgrade a home kitchen. You could really use the money to do some repairs on your truck and to buy some new equipment. The home owner says he'd like you to do the work, but is offering you 60,000 shares in Superfastgrowth.com in lieu of the $30,000.

In each case, the president of Superfastgrowth.com has given you the same pitch: "You'll make out like a bandit if you take my company's stock rather than cash. Sure, the stock market has had some big ups and downs, but we're about to receive $5 million of financing from Big Bucks venture capital firm, and we're on track to do an IPO (initial public offering) in a year, maybe two years if the market is soft. The stock, which the venture capital firm valued at 50 cents a share, could easily be worth $20 a share when it goes public. After that, who knows? You've seen what's happened to a lot of these Internet companies after they go public."

You're the graphic designer and your mind is racing, doing the calculations. At $20 a share, 20,000 shares would be worth $400,000. At $50 a share, those 20,000 shares would be worth . . . $1 million! The others are doing similar calculations. The Harvard MBA has just determined that at $50 a share, her 50,000 shares would be worth $2.5 million.

But the president of Superfastgrowth.com isn't a patient man. He's given you what he feels is a great deal, and he wants his answer now. Okay, maybe tomorrow. But if you wait any longer, the deal will likely change, he warns, and it won't change for the better for you.

What do you do? If you're like a growing number of Americans, you take the deal. That's because you've heard or read stories about ordinary people with companies like Microsoft, Dell, and hundreds of dot-coms who've struck it rich with employee stock options or newly issued stock. Who wouldn't want to duplicate such seemingly instant riches?

But do you know if accepting stock options in Superfastgrowth.com really is a good deal? How much of the founder's pitch should you believe? How can you find out what's possibly inaccurate or unfounded? Do you know if it's worth forfeiting a secure job and taking a pay cut? Do you know if it's worth foregoing a super job in an investment banking firm? Do you know if it's worth $30,000 of cash in construction payments . . . today?

It could be just a shot in the dark, or it could be a reasonable risk in a business climate where lots of companies have gone public and made everyone connected with them very wealthy. No less a business authority than Peter Drucker argues for the former. "Stock options play on the same old irrational expectations that drive an . . . immigrant to buy a lottery ticket," he told *Fortune* in 1998. "You know you're unlikely to win, but what's the risk?" The vice chairman of the holding company run by renowned investor Warren Buffett was quoted in *Inc.* magazine the same year as saying that options resemble "a chain letter."

I'm not one to take issue with such formidable authorities as Peter Drucker or Warren Buffett. Certainly there is an important element of chance connected with making out well with stock options. However, unlike the lottery or a chain letter, knowledge and information can help ordinary people improve the odds of success via stock options.

I've been on both sides of the stock option and equity game—I've received options and I've handed them out to employees of my company. I've discussed options as components of compensation plans in my previous books *(How to Really Start Your Own Business* and *How to Really Create a Successful Business Plan)*. While initially I viewed options much like Drucker—as akin to a lottery ticket, to be put aside and pulled out later to see if I had gotten lucky— I've changed my view. I've come to realize that options are in reality a currency with potentially huge value. I've personally profited from my options situations, and I've seen many other individuals profit, as well.

9

I've also come to realize that I might have profited even more than I did from using stock options. In the situations where I've received options, I might have negotiated even harder, and received more options on now-valuable shares than I did. When I handed out options, I might have communicated their potential value more effectively than I did to the employees who received the options—and possibly been able to hire the individuals at a lower salary in consideration. In other words, what you don't know about stock options and other forms of equity compensation can be costly.

Get the Answers

Unfortunately, there has not been an easy way to learn the stock option ropes, aside from paying $350-an-hour lawyers for advice—not a realistic approach for most job seekers. So I decided to use my experience and knowledge about this complex subject to write a book to guide job hunters and employees.

There are books designed to help companies establish employee stock option plans and other equity incentive programs. Until now, there hasn't been anything substantive and comprehensive for ordinary job seekers and employees. *Better Than Money* is the first book about equity incentives and rewards to be written from the recipient's viewpoint. It is intended to help you become knowledgeable about the use of equity in employment, and thereby improve your odds of achieving financial success via stock options and other equity incentives. It is about turning your experience with equity rewards from one that seems like playing the lottery to one that is more like making an investment.

This book is designed to help you accomplish several goals:

- Understand the lingo associated with stock options and other equity approaches so that you understand exactly what you are being told.
- Understand the thinking of entrepreneurs who are handing out equity incentives so that you can negotiate realistically.
- Gain an overview of equity opportunities available to employees, with major emphasis on stock options because they represent the most common equity opportunity.
- Develop a systematic approach to exploiting the opportunities created by the wider availability of stock options and other equity mechanisms.
- Ask the right questions of prospective and existing employers.
- Determine how much of your compensation you should accept in stock options.
- Balance the role of equity incentives with your overall career goals.
- Poke holes in employer pitches designed to sell you on stock options.
- Identify the areas you should negotiate to get the best possible deal.
- Avoid the most common pitfalls, which can lead to costly tax problems down the road.
- Value equity available to you via stock options later on, after you've begun your job.
- Learn to take advantage of "down periods" in the stock market or a company's stock so you can negotiate new options.
- Determine when to consider walking away from a job that is based heavily on stock options.
- Develop a strategy for making equity incentives part of your ongoing investment portfolio.

What's Not Here

There are several things you *won't* find in this book:

■ ***The technical details of employee stock option plans.*** The whole area of employee stock options and related equity programs can get quite complex, from a legal and tax perspective. I have tried to limit myself to the areas of stock option programs that directly affect benefits and value, so that you can develop your own personal strategy for handling specific situations. (I provide references to other resources at the end of the book.) If you have specific questions about a stock option arrangement you are considering or in which you are involved, your best sources for answers are an accountant, financial planner, and/or lawyer.

■ ***Lots of jargon.*** Not only are there many technicalities associated with employee stock options, there's also lots of jargon. You'll find some of it here, with definitions. As much as possible, however, I've tried to avoid jargon.

■ ***A get-rich-quick mentality.*** In the worlds of investing and entrepreneurship, there are no guarantees of success, much as some people would have you believe otherwise. Your challenge is to obtain the information you need and assess it as effectively as you can to make the best possible decision at the appropriate time. So you won't find endless stories about how people got rich with equity incentives, with the implication that if you can't get rich the same way, you must have some fatal flaw.

The wonderful thing about the world of equity incentives is that it's not a one-shot world. Because of the mobility of our workplace, you usually get more than one chance. And now, you won't have to learn about what it takes to maximize your success entirely via the school of hard knocks. ■

Chapter 1

A New Currency, and It's Not Money

Employers are no longer reluctant to share the potential future wealth of their enterprises. In order to build fast-growth businesses, they know they have to offer a piece of the company as "currency" to motivate talented people like you to come onboard. Six key trends are behind their newfound "religion."

T he notion of a collection of individuals owning part of a company (i.e. having equity, or stock) is a concept that has been around for several centuries. Until very recently, though, the only way to obtain equity was to start the company or to buy the equity. Even today, most people obtain equity by purchasing it via stock brokerage firms on stock markets like the New York Stock Exchange or NASDAQ.

And the notion of employers paying employees with cash is equally well established. There are examples from agrarian economies and earlier industrial days (i.e. Pullman towns) of employees being paid in food and shelter. But for most people in most parts of the world, compensation for work performed is paid in cash.

Increasingly, however, equity is being used as a currency by company founders and owners to compensate employees, outside contractors, and others. The most common compensation technique is payment of employee

13

stock options, which technically provide an opportunity to buy stock in your employer at a predetermined price. But the practice of handing out stock or the opportunity to buy stock is extending to other arenas. Some entrepreneurs have handed out stock to construction contractors or restaurant owners in payment for goods and services. Others have extended the opportunity to business associates to buy stock in their companies—invariably at the attractive offering price—on the day the companies go public, and then soar in value. And still others have granted to their lawyers and other professional service providers options or warrants (a cousin of options) as part of their payment for services.

Traditionally, owners of private companies have been quite reluctant to part with equity. Individuals start companies partly to create their own fiefdoms. Few kings want to share control of their fiefdoms. Nor do many want to share the wealth they expect from the venture. So what's going on as we enter a new millennium? Is human nature suddenly changing? Not by a long shot. The emergence of equity as a compensation currency is a reflection of significant historical, social, and economic changes that have occurred over just a few years.

My Fantasy vs. An Entrepreneur's Reality

I have witnessed some of these changes firsthand over the last thirty-plus years, including one that has played out over a period of more than twenty years. I had this fantasy during the years I spent as an employee during the 1970s and 1980s that I would sign on as an editor with a smart publishing entrepreneur, get a small piece of the company in exchange, and enjoy the ride to riches.

Back in the spring of 1978, when I was exploring the possibility of leaving my job as a staff reporter with *The Wall Street Journal* for an editing position, I thought I had discovered the opportunity about which I'd dreamed. I learned about a Boston magazine publisher, Bernie Goldhirsh, who had successfully built a sailing magazine, and was about to launch a magazine directed at small businesses. We had lunch, and he told me about his magazine, which he had decided to name *Inc.*

It sounded very exciting—targeting an underserved marketplace and being launched by a publisher with substantial financial resources and a clear focus on what he wanted to accomplish. Still, it was risky, as all magazines are. And this was at a time when far fewer new companies were being launched than are now.

So when Bernie expressed interest in hiring me as an editor (exact title and duties undefined), I inquired about the possibility of being able to obtain some small ownership in the enterprise—not only to fulfill my fantasy, but to compensate me (psychologically, and hopefully financially) for leaving a secure, prestigious position in exchange for a job that was way down the totem pole in both areas. Bernie is a thoughtful guy who has always seemed to me to bear a resemblance to Dustin Hoffman. He looked at me quizzically and said, "That's something I may consider at some point in the future. But not now."

Bernie's response put me off enough that I set aside my fantasy and went with Option 2: becoming an associate editor at *The Harvard Business Review*. Of course, *Inc.* went on to become a major business magazine. After seven years at *HBR*, I left to become a senior editor at, of all places, *Inc.* magazine. At that point, I was told by the editors who hired me, stock still wasn't being made available to employees at *Inc.* But, of course, the risk of joining *Inc.* at that point in its existence was much lower than it had been in 1978.

I stayed at *Inc.* for only a year, deciding in 1986 to launch my own marketing communications business. But I remained in touch with a number of employees there, and when I'd speak with them, I'd inquire as to whether Bernie

15

had changed his approach to making stock available. They'd usually laugh.

The laughing stopped in late 1999, when Bernie announced that he was spinning off the online version of *Inc.* to form a new company, Inc.com. In this venture, key employees were given stock options that could potentially have significant value if and when the new enterprise goes public or is sold. It had taken Bernie more than 20 years, but he had finally come around to face the inevitable: Employee stock options are a prerequisite for entrepreneurs intending to build fast-growth businesses—a new currency that increasing numbers of people now view as better than money.

Nor was Bernie alone. It used to be that one or several entrepreneurs owned all the stock of the companies they founded or acquired. This is no longer the case. According to data collected by Segal Co., a New York benefits consulting firm, founders of companies with less than $10 million of annual sales are being forced to give up increasing amounts of stock to outsiders. It found that from 1996 to 1998, the average stock holding by the CEOs or presidents (usually the founders or owners) of such companies had declined from 48% to 39%, as incentive compensation given to "rank and file" employees increased.

The Beginning of the Real Story

For prospective and existing employees of Inc.com, gaining access to potentially valuable stock options is not the end of the story. In fact, it's only the beginning. Anyone trying to determine the value of a job at Inc.com must ascribe value to the stock options that come with the job or a job offer. Making that determination is no easy task, even for business professionals. It is especially difficult when the enterprise is privately held, as Inc.com was at the beginning of 2000.

16

Around the country, thousands of people are regularly being called on to make determinations about job offers that include stock options. For most, it is a judgment call they must make in a vacuum, partly because it is such a recent addition to the world of work and partly because there is little information to educate employees.

It is important to understand what is going on here so that when you are offered stock options, you understand their real import—that they aren't just some gift that has fallen from the sky, or just another benefit. As my experience with Bernie Goldhirsh suggests, company owners don't hand out ownership in their companies the same way they hand out health insurance or vacation pay. Stock options for ordinary employees are a very recent phenomenon, and are evidence of a complete turnaround in what some might call "the paradigm" of work.

The Forces at Work

What's behind the changed paradigm of work? A number of simultaneously occurring trends are driving the new vision of work and the use of equity incentives:

■ *The boom in the stock market, which began in 1982.* Since then, all indexes have soared, with just a few off years; the Dow Jones Industrial Average has shot up from less than 1,000 to more than 11,000 at times in late 1999 and early 2000. Why is a booming stock market so important? Because it has the effect of making many companies' shares more valuable than they might have been in earlier decades. This enables companies to use their stock rather than cash as "currency" to make acquisitions and to recruit and incentivize the most talented employees.

■ *The growing importance of people in business (rather than machines or real estate).* For increasing numbers of businesses, knowledge and information are the key success factors, and they come only from people. Bill

17

Gates has been widely and frequently quoted about how the key to Microsoft's success has been its focus on hiring the smartest, most talented people it can find. People, of course, need to be motivated, and stock options have become a motivational fuel.

■ *The growing competition for people.* In an economy where knowledge and information are so important, people become the critical resource. And in an increasing number of industries, people with the right skills are in short supply. About 850,000 information technology jobs will go unfilled during 2000, the Information Technology Association of America predicted in a study early in the same year. The laws of supply and demand inevitably drive up the prices for people. For companies short of cash, stock becomes a way to fill in potential pay gaps.

■ *The rise of the Internet.* Its primary impact on the use of equity incentives is to distribute information about job opportunities, letting individuals easily understand the dynamics of the job market. Employees can quickly determine if their current job situation compares favorably with others out there, and if not, they can easily search out other situations, presumably with more attractive equity opportunities. (Additionally, the Internet has spawned huge numbers of new companies.)

■ *A free ride from policy makers.* When companies pay cash for salaries, bonuses, and benefits, there is an immediate impact on profits and cash flow. When they issue stock options, the impact is almost negligible. There is no penalty on profits or cash flow. Yes, public companies must disclose information about equity in their filings with the Securities and Exchange Commission, and provide some footnotes in their financial statements. When one policy making organization—the American Institute of Certified Public Accountants (AICPA)—tried in the mid-1990s to

18

force companies to reflect the impact of stock options on their balance sheets, there was a near revolt among high-tech companies, and the idea was dropped. Stock options don't show up in any of the economic indicators the federal government uses to measure inflation. The federal government's only significant involvement with equity compensation is to tax it, but this comes after the value has been received, not before. So businesses really have had a "free ride" from policy makers in using equity compensation as currency.

■ *Significant tax breaks.* During a time when many professionals have seen themselves paying an effective tax rate in the neighborhood of 40%-plus (taking into account federal withholding, FICA, Medicare, state income taxes), any opportunity to save on taxes becomes quite attractive. That helps explain the rapid rise of IRA and 401(k) retirement plans. Well, stock options can offer their own version of tax benefits. As I discuss in more detail later, stock options are really a type of compensation, but they aren't taxed as such. For one thing, they aren't taxed when they're awarded. Also, certain types of options (discussed later) aren't taxed when exercised. And if the stock acquired via options is held for at least a year, the gains from selling the stock are taxed at a maximum federal rate of only 20%.

None of these trends shows any immediate sign of changing in a way that could adversely affect the use of equity compensation. The two that are most prone to change are the booming stock market (which showed increasing volatility through the early months of 2000) and the free ride from policy makers. Anytime a benefit becomes seemingly too good to be true, there tends to be either a marketplace or regulatory backlash. ■

Chapter 2

You're Not Only An Employee, You're an Investor

In today's economy, a job is much more than a job. It is also an investment. As such, you need to begin thinking like an investor as you assess job opportunities. Understand what you're investing in if you take a particular job—and the risks you're incurring. The opportunities and risks change according to the stage at which you become involved with a particular company.

O nce upon a time, people took jobs to earn a living. Almost since the beginning of time, work has generally been viewed as a privilege for the employee. After all, a job provides you with the money you need to put food on the table, a roof over your head and, if you're really lucky, a little leftover money for fun and recreation on Saturday night. In the last few centuries, if individuals wanted to make a lot more money than they could in a job, and possibly get rich, they started their own businesses.

Conventional wisdom has it that when an employer offers you a job, the employer is "making an investment" in you. Rarely has the converse been considered: that when you accept a job, you are making an investment in the employer—of your time, energy, knowledge, creativity, and innovativeness.

21

Increasingly, though, the conventional wisdom is changing. It is changing as employers come to realize that labor, which during Industrial Age days was viewed as a cheap commodity, is now, during the Information Age, likely to be a company's most precious asset. The reason is that knowledge is the great driver of business success during the Information Age, and knowledge comes from people.

Work as an Investment

I helped found an Internet services company, and as we grew between 1995 and 1999, I learned the hard way about the value and importance of the programmers, content developers, and salespeople we hired. At one point in early 1999, we lost three of our eleven employees to other companies that made them super-attractive offers—all in a span of two weeks. In the black humor that followed that episode, whenever an unpleasant issue came up during a management meeting or other get-together of the remaining employees, someone would invariably blurt out, "I quit!"

The lesson to me from that unfortunate period was that employees wield an awesome amount of power. Very fundamentally, when individuals decided to accept jobs at our company, they were making an investment in it. The three employees who departed made a determination, for whatever reasons, that the investments they had made in the company weren't producing the returns they wanted or expected, and so decided to invest their assets (themselves) elsewhere. And the hot job market of the late 1990s made it very easy for them to seek out other investments.

While these particular employees might not have thought about their situations in exactly those terms, you should. Where do you want to invest this precious asset (yourself)? What kind of a return do you expect on the investment? Over how long a period of time? Those are the kinds of questions every investor asks about the money he or she is about to invest.

Keep in mind, also, that when you make an investment, you take a risk. Generally speaking, the greater the risk, the greater the potential rewards. What this means in real life is that the earlier in the growth stage of a company you invest, the riskier the investment. From a job perspective, the earlier you get involved in a company's growth, the more cash strapped the company is likely to be, and therefore the more receptive it will be to handing out stock options (in place of cash).

Conversely, if you receive options in a publicly-held company, your risk is somewhat reduced because the company is well established, but so generally is your "upside" potential compared to an early-stage, privately-held company. The risk is less because you can look up the company's stock price and quickly tabulate the potential value of the options. Because the value is known in the public marketplace, it is unlikely to increase by the same order of magnitude as an early-stage company; few public companies increase in value 500 times over the course of a couple of years, as some private technology companies have done in recent years.

In the world of stock options, the preceding translates as follows: You'll find a company's generosity with equity greatest in its early days, and you'll see the generosity decline over time as the company becomes more successful. The early bird really does tend to get the worms, if it's willing to put up with the risks of unknown predators.

Improving Your Odds

Amazingly, there is a way to actually reduce the risk of being there early: having the right information. The more information you have about the company in which you want to invest yourself, the better you will be able to assess the nature of the risk. Understanding and assessing the risk won't eliminate it (nothing can). But having enough information can help you make an informed decision, which is a much different approach than buying a lottery ticket. You may decide that the risk is unacceptable. If you do decide to jump in, at least you'll be going in with your eyes fully open.

One of the beautiful things about the employee as an investor is that you don't have to risk money. Rather, you risk your time and energy. In the world of entrepreneurship, your time and energy have long had the label of "sweat equity." There's a tendency to value sweat equity less than money from an investment perspective, but it isn't insignificant because it comes with two costs:

1. *Opportunity cost.* The time you spend working for Employer A is time you don't have for Employer B, C, or D, even if they offer a superior return on investment. You want to maximize the odds that Employer A will offer a return on your investment superior to Employer B, C, and D, where you may have turned down job offers.

2. *Salary cost.* In certain situations, especially involving early-stage private companies, employees are asked to forego a "market" salary in exchange for stock options. Thus, if you are paid a $50,000 annual salary plus stock options instead of the $70,000 you could command somewhere else, you are essentially investing $20,000 annually for the privilege of receiving stock options. It's as if you are writing a check for $20,000 a year to work at the lower-salary company.

In today's Information Age, which is increasingly fueled by human knowledge rather than by gasoline, coal, or people-based assembly lines, the potential return on your time and energy investment is huge. It comes in the form of stock options and other opportunities for obtaining equity. In today's New World of Work, your challenge is to minimize your opportunity and salary cost, and maximize your return on investment.

A Special Kind of Investment

When it comes to approaches for investing, there are seemingly endless books that provide guidance about risk versus reward. And there are as many formulas for investing as there are diets for losing weight.

If you want to understand approaches for evaluating stock for investing, it might be worth reviewing some of these books. But when it comes to investing yourself in a company, there is one factor that makes it different from all other kinds of investments: *it is a job.*

The title of this chapter is meant to make a dual point: that you need to understand your new role in your job as an investor, but also not lose sight of the fact that this investment is also your job. Work, after all, is where you spend more time than just about anything else you do. You want to enjoy it (or at least a good chunk of it). You want to learn from it. You want opportunity for advancement. You want benefits like health insurance and tuition reimbursement. And you want to earn money (i.e. cash paid out every week or two weeks) from it.

Obviously, the long-term quality of the job is less important if you are a consultant or other service provider, and you are receiving stock or options for performing a particular service. That's because the service will be something you are likely providing part-time and for a limited time period. But if you are in a position of receiving stock options as part of a new job, you need to strike a balance—satisfying yourself that the company is a promising investment and the job is a job that will do what a job is supposed to do.

The balance should be comfortable for you. Comfort will vary from person to person. Part of the challenge in striking the right balance is understanding yourself as an investor and as an employee. I explore this issue more fully in Chapter 5, which poses the question, "What Kind of an Employee Investor Are You?" Before you can assess yourself effectively, you need to understand the terrain on which you'll be operating, so the next two chapters examine the realities and lingo you'll be called on to take into account. ■

Chapter 3

Can You Really Get Rich Working for Someone Else?

It's only been in recent years that we've been able to give a positive answer to this chapter's title. The perception, however, has grown that it's easy to get rich via stock options, and of late we've seen Harvard Business School graduates jumping in record numbers to work for low wages at high-tech firms offering stock options. The reality is that only small percentages of those signing on to promising tech companies are making out. It's important to separate hype from reality, and here's how to get started.

C onventional wisdom has long had it that you can't get rich working for someone else, that the only legal ways to make a fortune are to start your own business, buy a hot stock, or win the lottery. But attitudes have changed radically in recent years. Witness two related incidents:

***

In late 1999, *The Boston Globe* classifieds featured a quarter-page ad from an e-commerce software company, EC Cubed, seeking software engineers, developers, technical writers, and others.

"Opportunity. Growth. Equity. Get all three at EC Cubed," screamed the heading. The statements about opportunity and growth were fairly predictable stuff about how fast the company was growing and how "you'll go as far as your career aspirations will take you." But under "Equity," the ad was a little different: "Ah, the rewards. At the end of the day, EC Cubed employees know they've earned—and own—a piece of the company's success. With unlimited opportunity, explosive growth and generous benefits, including pre-IPO stock options, there really is no better time to join EC Cubed."

***

At just about the same time as that ad came out, a good friend of mine—a stay-at-home mom and freelance writer—told me she had taken an editorial management job with a young, fast-growing company that supplies news over the Internet. Janet (not her real name) is one of the more risk-averse people I know, and I've known her for 25 years. She's mostly avoided the stock market and when she's held jobs, they've always been with major corporations able to provide the benefits and stability she so values.

So here she was at age 50, signing on with an insecure Internet startup. I couldn't resist asking her, "Did you get any stock options?"

"Ah, the magic words," she replied. "Equity participation."

The Power of Perception

These incidents don't answer the question posed as this chapter's title. In fact, they may convey misleading information; for example, as I discuss in Chapter 6, the pre-IPO stock alluded to in the newspaper ad can be much less attractive than is popularly believed. But these incidents begin to answer another question: Are people willing to try to get rich working for someone else? The answer is a resounding yes. More and more people are willing to believe that the answer to this chapter's title question has changed,

28

and companies are playing into that change in a big way so as to lure top people.

As we all know, perception is often more important than reality in determining people's beliefs and actions. The current perception is being fueled by the newspaper and magazine articles describing the experiences of ordinary people who are getting wealthy via stock options.

Even supposedly savvy employees like Harvard Business School graduates are joining the rush to options. By 1999, the percentage of Harvard MBAs taking jobs in high technology, where options are most prevalent, had doubled to 18% from four years earlier. The percentage going into consulting, long the most popular job destination for Harvard B-School grads, had declined 24% during the same period. In an article entitled, "McKinsey Who?" *Forbes* magazine described a graduate of UCLA's business school who turned down offers from two top consulting firms, including one with a $140,000 salary, to go with an Internet startup offering a $75,000 salary and 50,000 shares in options; in a public offering, that individual could be worth $1 million if the shares hit $20 each.

A Historical Perspective

We Americans generally don't like to spend a great deal of time studying history. We'd rather believe that we're the first generation to experience a phenomenon like a stock market boom or a particularly difficult war, or whatever. But more often than not, we can learn from history, and so it is with stock options.

Stock options have a checkered history, and are certainly much more prevalent now than ever before. But they've had their ups and downs. During the 1950s and 1960s, corporate boards of directors—spurred by Congress' liberalization on taxation of capital gains realized from stock sales—began granting options, but only to the most senior executives. The grants were usually fairly modest by today's standards—perhaps up to 2,500 shares annually. Today's top corporate executives frequently have options on several hundred thousand or even a few million shares of stock.

When the stock market tailed off during the late 1960s and 1970s, interest in stock options evaporated, since the profits had gone out of stocks. By the late 1970s and 1980s, though, stock options for senior executives came back into vogue in a much bigger way. A watershed event was the hiring by a financially wobbly Chrysler Corp. of Lee Iacocca from Ford Motor Co. in 1978—with the big lure being options to buy 400,000 shares of Chrysler stock at a low price.

Other companies large and small took the hint and began using options to attract top executives, especially on the West Coast. During the 1980s, startups like Sun Microsystems, Microsoft, and Oracle Corp. offered generous option deals in place of large salaries to key employees—and made them rich when the companies went public.

The experiences of the technology startups, together with the leveraged buyouts that became popular during the 1980s, convinced many executives that the best way to get rich working for someone else was to own equity rather than to negotiate large salaries and bonuses. By the 1990s, options had become the norm for senior executives, and had spread far outside the executive suite to ordinary employees. By spring of 2000, when stock markets experienced sharp swings up and down, some business media wondered whether the wide acceptance of stock options might be in danger. The following reports and studies indicate how far the trend has spread:

■ At least seven million employees are eligible to receive stock options, according to a 1999 National Center for Employee Ownership (NCEO) estimate, based on its analysis of research studies that NCEO and other organizations conducted.

■ About 30% of America's 350 largest companies provide options to a large segment of their employees, according to a 1997 survey by William M. Mercer, an executive consulting firm.

■ Just over half of public companies using stock option plans grant stock options to all employees, according to a 1997 survey by ShareData Inc. and the American Electronics Association (AEA).

■ Two-thirds of technology companies make stock options available to all employees, *Inc.* magazine reported in 1999.

■ In the Internet industry, 62% of CEO compensation came in the form of stock options during 1999, versus 36% in large corporations, reported Spencer Stuart, an executive search firm, based on a study of 480 Internet executives. According to the firm, Internet companies "have wholeheartedly embraced stock options and turned them into a compensation mantra—options, options, options."

The Hype

Is it really possible for the so-called "average" employee to become rich working for someone else? All kinds of anecdotal evidence exists to support the idea. The media over the last few years have been full of stories of people who have made huge amounts of money from stock options.

You've likely read at least some of these stories. Among the most popular have been stories about the "Microsoft millionaires"—the hundreds of Microsoft employees who received Microsoft stock options during the company's formative years in the 1980s and emerged as millionaires in the 1990s.

31

BusinessWeek reported about Heather Beach who, at age 25, took a $7,000 pay cut from a previous employer to accept a receptionist job in 1993 with Siebel Systems Inc. in East Palo Alto, CA, and by 1997 was a millionaire, thanks to stock options and additional stock she took as part of her pay. The same magazine told the story of Jennifer Overstreet, who worked for twelve years as the personal assistant to Oracle Corp.'s CEO and by 1996 was so wealthy she quit her job to fix up an 8,000-square-foot home in San Francisco's Pacific Heights.

In *The Wall Street Journal* was the tale of Paul Hansen, a Berkeley, CA, building contractor who did about $30,000 worth of construction work—erecting walls, installing windows, and putting in a kitchen—for an Internet startup in 1998. The company persuaded Hansen to take stock rather than cash. You can guess the rest of the story: By late 1999, the stock was worth nearly $600,000.

The Reality

We all know that the media feasts on rags-to-riches stories (as well as riches-to-rags stories). Indeed, the media is full of "exceptions" and "accidents" (literally and figuratively). Media stories about ordinary people striking it rich in the California Gold Rush of the mid-1800s were instrumental in helping to settle the West. Unfortunately, most of the real riches made during that period were by companies like Levi Strauss that sold supplies to the hordes of people that descended on California in search of riches. The vast majority of the people digging for gold found nothing but disappointment.

When you look at the hard numbers in the world of business, you realize that the lessons of the Gold Rush still have applicability. For starters, consider the fact that more than one million new businesses are started every year. Fewer than 10,000 of those raise venture capital, and fewer than 1,000 of those are destined to go public. And of the 600-800 that have been going public each year, only a fraction of those will achieve stock performance on a par with Microsoft or Dell. If it seems like a pretty tight screen, it is.

What happens to the options held by employees at the companies that don't "make it"? Well, the stock in some of those companies rises sharply in value when the company is acquired. But for the employees of many others, the opportunity and salary costs they incur aren't compensated for with rapidly rising stock prices. Instead, they turn into real costs as the companies struggle and may even go out of business.

Of course, every individual who takes a job with a supposedly "hot" new Internet or biotech company hopes he or she will be different. I've met a number of such individuals. I remember one in particular—Gary, a smartly styled 40-year-old with carefully groomed graying hair, whom I interviewed as a potential sales executive with my Internet company. He was the Eastern sales manager of a video streaming company, which had raised $14 million or so from venture capitalists over the previous few years. But its technology had been upstaged by a large technology company, which was giving it away for free. Gary's company had avoided the mergers and partnerships of some of its competitors. Now it was out there alone, and in trouble. Gary wanted to bail out.

Bailing out meant more than just leaving a job. He had access to about 3% of the company's stock if he decided to purchase his options. Unfortunately, he judged, likely correctly, that the stock had little chance of achieving any significant value.

It was sad listening to him describe the situation. He had started out with such high hopes. And he was clearly despondent about the lost opportunity. In his view, not

33

surprisingly, the problem lay with other executives who had refused to listen to his advice. Whatever the real circumstances, Gary was looking at three years of his "investment" time and reduced salary cost about to go down the drain, and having to start over. We didn't hire him, but more than likely he took a new job with new options, and new hopes and dreams.

What could Gary have done differently? Certainly he could have entered the options game with much more knowledge than it seems he did. More about the game in the next chapter. ■

Chapter 4

Here's the Game

Entrepreneurs who need your talents often know how to play on your hopes for quick riches. Here's Johnny Sweetalker's technique—the lingo and thinking he uses to attract eager employee candidates. By understanding his game, you'll learn important lessons about looking (and what to look for) before you leap.

I f you're going to seriously assess equity incentives, and stock options in particular, you need to familiarize yourself with the lingo. Too often, prospective employees sit at a job interview listening to a company executive talk about "incentive and nonqualified stock options," "vesting periods," "strike price," and "dilution," and just nod their heads as if they understand everything.

While the basic goal of equity incentives is fairly straightforward (buy low, sell high), the accompanying lingo is complicated and often communicates subtle yet very important messages—such as, for instance, whether you really can acquire the stock to which you think you're entitled when you expect to acquire it. The lingo reflects the assorted legal and tax rules that are part of stock option plans and other equity incentives.

Rather than try to provide a technical explanation of the terminology, I put together a composite story to help

35

clarify the lingo. You'll see key terminology in bold type. And you'll find a glossary of terms at the end of the book.

Tale of a New Company

Once upon a time, right around the turn of the century, twenty-something Johnnie Sweetalker started a company, Superfastgrowth.com. It would be a "different" kind of online mall making use of some special software Johnny had conceived but not yet fully developed. Because Johnnie was using his own savings, along with credit card loans, to get the company going, he figured he couldn't afford to pay competitive salaries for the programmers, salespeople, consultants, and executives he knew he'd need, and whom he knew were in short supply.

So he decided that a good way to get people to join his company and keep them motivated without paying them competitive salaries would be to set up a **stock option plan**. Johnnie went for assistance to a lawyer who specialized in compensation issues for technology-oriented companies.

The lawyer asked Johnnie a few questions. First, he wanted to know how many shares Superfastgrowth.com had outstanding, and how many were authorized. Johnny told the lawyer that Superfastgrowth had 500,000 **shares outstanding** and fifteen million **shares authorized**.

"Here's my first piece of advice," the lawyer stated. "Increase the number of shares outstanding—the number you and the other shareholders actually own—to five million. You can do that by splitting your shares—for each share you own, you'll get nine more, for a total of 4,500,000 new shares. Add that to the 500,000 you have, and you have five million. That way, you can hand out **option grants** of 10,000, 50,000, or even a few hundred thousand shares at a time to employees, and the shares will represent just a small piece of the company. People like big numbers rather than small numbers. They'd rather get 50,000 shares at 10 cents a share than 5,000 shares at $1 a share, even though the value is exactly the same. There's a psychological factor here. Don't ask me exactly why it's like that, but it is." If Superfastgrowth.com ever needed to issue additional shares, such as to venture capitalists or other investors, it would have a reserve of ten million **authorized shares** that could be issued by a vote of the board of directors. However, the lawyer warned Johnnie that issuing additional shares and thereby increasing the number of shares outstanding down the road would have the effect of **diluting**, or reducing the value of, the shares of holders of the five million original shares outstanding.

Next, the lawyer wanted to know what kind of options Johnnie wanted to make available to employees, contractors, and others he wanted to motivate. He explained to Johnnie that two types of options are most commonly used: **incentive stock options (ISOs)** and **nonqualified stock options (NSOs)**. Incentive stock options qualify for preferential tax treatment—the key preference being that the recipient can delay paying taxes on stock acquired by **exercising** the option until the stock is actually sold. If the recipient sells the stock right away, any gain is treated as **ordinary income**, which gets taxed at the same rate as your salary; but if the stock is held for a year, any gain qualifies as a **capital gain**, which is taxed at a maximum of 20%.

But, he added, incentive stock options can only be granted to employees (as opposed to consultants or other contractors). Nonqualified options can be handed out to consultants, contractors, outside directors, and anyone else the company wants, but the recipient pays taxes on the difference between the exercise price of the option and the value of the shares as ordinary income as soon as the shares are acquired, rather than when the shares are sold. That means the recipient may wind up paying taxes before receiving any money.

Johnny had another question. "I keep hearing about **restricted stock**. What is it, and should I be offering it?"

"Restricted stock can best be thought of as a mirror image of incentive stock options," the lawyer said. "Instead of being made available for purchase over time, as incentive stock options are, restricted stock is given out all at once when an individual joins a company, usually with the restriction that it be sold or given back to the company if the employee leaves before a certain amount of time has gone by. The reason more companies are making restricted stock available to certain senior executives is that it offers a potential tax advantage: Because executives get their hands on the stock as soon as they join the company, they have a good shot at fulfilling the one-year holding period necessary to qualify for capital gains treatment on any profits from the eventual sale of the stock. And given how quickly some fast-growth companies are going public or being acquired, the capital gains treatment can result in significant tax savings."

"That leads to another question," Johnny said. "What about me? Can I participate in the stock option program?"

"You certainly can, since you're an employee," the lawyer said. "I'd be inclined if I were you to wait a year or two to see how the company does and how long the options designated in your plan will last. You'd like them to last at least three or four years before having to increase the number of shares further. But for you to be able to acquire some of your company's stock via options isn't a bad idea, since right now you have **founders stock**, which you will likely be prohibited from selling for some period of time after an **initial public offering** or acquisition."

"One more thing," Johnny said. "What about **phantom stock**? I've heard that it's a way to give stock to employees without giving them voting rights."

"Yes, phantom stock is just what the name implies. It's stock that isn't really stock at the moment it's issued, but

38

can be converted into real stock under certain circumstances, such as when a company is sold, or when the phantom stock shareholders reach a certain age. It's used a lot by family companies to pass ownership to the younger generation, without the founders giving up authority. But it's more complicated to put together a phantom stock program than a conventional stock option program, since there are more legalities surrounding the rights of holders and the circumstances under which phantom stock turns into real stock. And phantom stock tends not to qualify for favorable tax treatment. Besides, employees today are smart enough to question phantom programs and demand the real thing, which is stock through an option program."

Johnny decided to accept his lawyer's advice. He rejected the phantom stock approach, and agreed to offer both incentive and nonqualified stock options in Superfastgrowth.com's stock option plan. He also had his lawyer handle the paperwork necessary for Johnny to be able to offer restricted stock, if necessary, to attract a key executive.

The next major question from the lawyer was about how many shares Johnny wanted to make available under the stock option plan. He explained to Johnny that growth companies like Superfastgrowth.com typically set aside options for between 10% and 20% of their outstanding shares for stock option plans. Anything much less than 10% likely wouldn't make enough shares available to employees to make them feel as if they were truly owners, the lawyer explained. Johnny decided to set aside 900,000 shares, which when added to the 5 million already outstanding, represented nearly 15% of the company's **fully diluted capitalization** (5.9 million shares).

There were a number of other technical issues that he explained to Johnny, but the final major issue concerned the **exercise price** of the options. This was a major question because it needed to be related to the actual value of the company, while also serving as an incentive to recipients. In other words, the price need to be as low as possible, without being so ridiculously low that the Internal Revenue Service could challenge it sometime in the future.

But, Johnny wanted to know, how could he apply a value to Superfastgrowth.com at such an early stage?

"Well, think about it this way," the lawyer advised. "If I were a venture capitalist interested in investing in Superfastgrowth.com, how much would you tell me it's worth?"

Johnny thought for a moment. "Well, there's the Web site design I've done, there's the software that's in beta testing, but most of all, there's the concept. And my marketing tests have all shown that people want to buy products our new way. Given how Internet companies have been valued, I'd say we're worth at least $5 million at this point."

"Fine," said the lawyer. "Now, imagine I'm your wife's divorce lawyer, and I'm trying to arrive at a settlement with you about how much you should compensate her for half of Superfastgrowth.com, since she doesn't want stock. For how much would you value your company?" Johnny didn't have to think long. "Gee, we're just a startup, with no sales, no employees. It's just a concept. Who knows how long this Internet bubble is going to last? Maybe $400,000 or $500,000."

"Great," said the lawyer. "You've just come up with the exercise price. This is generally the lowest possible price that still has credibility in the marketplace. If the company could be considered to have a value of $500,000, then with five million shares outstanding, you'd have a price of 10 cents a share. This is the amount your new employees will have to pay if and when they decide to **exercise options** and buy the stock."

The lawyer wasn't through, however. "Once you raise investment funds from venture capitalists, the process for valuing options will change further. The reason is that the venture capitalists will almost certainly demand that they receive **preferred stock** instead of **common stock** in return for their investment funds. As the name implies, preferred stock has certain preferences over common stock. Holders of preferred stock may have the power to name a certain number of directors, to be repaid all their investment if the company encounters financial difficulties, to have the voting power to name a new chief executive, and other such special privileges."

"So, what does all that have to do with valuation?" asked Johnny.

"Well, in exchange for such preferences, the preferred shares carry a higher valuation than the common shares. If Superfastgrowth.com issues 2 million preferred shares to venture capitalists, in addition to its 5 million common shares, it could be that the preferred shares are valued at $2.50 a share and the common shares at 10 cents a share. That would make the preferred shares worth $5 million, and the common shares worth $500,000, for a total company valuation of $5.5 million. That would allow you to continue issuing stock options at 10 cents a share, even after you've received investment funds."

Johnny looked puzzled. "But the common shareholders would seem to be at a serious disadvantage, since the preferred shareholders are calling all the shots."

"Yes, they do," the lawyer answered. "But if the company grows quickly and is a candidate for an IPO or a high-priced acquisition, then the preferred shareholders will vote to convert their stock into common shares so that everyone will receive the same high price for public shares or a high acquisition price. That's when common shares really increase sharply in value."

41

The First Employee
That afternoon

Johnny was starting to like this idea of stock options more than he ever thought he would. Options might actually help him recruit the hotshot computer programmer he was interviewing at 3 p.m.—the one his friend who had referred the programmer had told him "is probably out of your league financially."

It didn't take Johnny more than about 15 minutes to decide that he wanted to hire the programmer, Jeff. He was in his mid-20s and had been into programming since he was in high school. Yes, his black hair was tied in a ponytail, he had a silver earring in one ear, and he looked as if he had slept in the gray suit he was wearing, but he had spent the last three years doing Internet-related programming for a large corporation—just the kind of programming that Johnny wanted done. Jeff was tired of the impersonal nature of corporate life, and wanted to sign on with a smaller company, where he could be more creative, and make money by getting his hands on some stock.

However, Jeff hadn't thought about signing on with a company quite as small as Superfastgrowth.com. "I've actually been talking to a few other companies," he told Johnny. "I expect that at least two of them will make offers to me."

Johnny had read about how tight the labor market was for computer programmers, but here was the problem staring him in the face. "How much are you looking to earn?" Johnny asked, with a lump starting to form in his throat.

"I'm earning $45,000 in my current job. I'd like to go to $60,000," Jeff answered. "Plus, I'd like to be able to get some stock options, wherever I go."

Johnny tried to hide his gulp and hold his smile. Here was a kid in his twenties expecting to make $60,000 a year.

It seemed ludicrous. But Johnny thought about how getting Jeff onboard would help him jump-start his Web development work. He decided to make his pitch. "Would you like to get very rich, Jeff?"

Now Jeff was the one squirming a bit. "Sure, wouldn't everyone?"

"Do you know the story of the Microsoft Millionaires?"

"Not exactly," Jeff said. "I do know that a lot of employees got rich at Microsoft."

"Yes, that's true," said Johnny. "But the earliest employees at Microsoft got super rich. Others who came later made a lot of money, but didn't make anywhere near the millions the first ones made. That's the way it is, Jeff. The earliest employees stand to make the most money on stock options because they're taking the most risk."

"So what are you proposing?" Jeff asked.

"That you join Superfastgrowth.com and get rich," Johnny answered. "Here's the deal: I can't pay you what those other guys are going to be offering you. I can only offer you $30,000 a year. That's probably enough to meet your expenses. But I'll also grant you options on 50,000 shares, at 10 cents a share. Now let me give you a little inside information, Jeff. I'm going to be raising $5 million of venture capital. Once that happens, the company will probably have a value of more than $10 million, which could translate into something approaching $2 a share. That would make your shares worth more than $100,000, which translates into the equivalent of $130,000 of compensation your first year. And you won't be done, Jeff. Those shares will go up from there, just like Microsoft's did. And if you're doing a good job, I'll be granting you additional stock options. You may be able to retire before you're 30."

Jeff was silent for a moment. "Make it 100,000 shares, and you've got a deal."

Johnny replied instantly. "Why don't we split the difference, Jeff? I'll give you options on 75,000 shares."

Jeff reached across the table and shook Johnny's hand. "It's a deal."

As Jeff walked out of Johnny's office, the founder breathed a sigh of relief as he reached for the phone to dial his lawyer's number and request that he draw up an **option agreement** offering Jeff the options. Johnny told the lawyer about the negotiating session.

The lawyer had a few questions. "Did you tell him about the **vesting period**—that he'll have **cliff vesting** for the first year, meaning he will have to wait a year before he's eligible to acquire any stock, and then he will only get to acquire 25% of the options? After that, he will have **incremental vesting**, whereby he will be able to acquire shares each quarter—6.25% per quarter, or 25% per year. Does he understand that if he leaves or is fired after working for you two years, he'll only be able to buy half the shares in his option agreement?"

"He didn't ask," Johnny said.

"Well, you can still change the vesting approach by **accelerating** his options so he can acquire all his stock if you have an **initial public offering (IPO)** or even if he meets some performance target, like completing development of your major product on schedule or ahead of schedule."

"No, let's leave it the way it is," said Johnny. "I want people committed for the long term. And Jeff is so excited that I don't think he'll care."

Real Money, and Real Value
Six months later

Superfastgrowth.com has seven employees working in cramped offices located above a dry cleaner in a strip mall. It's late on a Thursday afternoon when Johnny calls everyone together to make an announcement.

"I've got some very good news," he says. "We've just completed an agreement to raise $10 million in a first round of venture capital. We were only looking to raise $5 million, but the investors think that our approach to selling online is truly revolutionary and could change the way business is done on the Internet. So they wanted to be sure we had enough money to do all the things that need doing. First and most immediately, we'll be able to move from these offices."

A mock cheer erupts from the small group. "Yes, I know you'll all miss the fumes from the dry cleaner," Johnny smiles. "Second, and more important, we'll be able to hire more people to get all the work done, and we'll be able to do some serious advertising and public relations to get our name out there."

Jeff pipes up. "What about our stock options? What kind of value do they now have?"

"I'm glad you asked," Johnny says. "Based on the investment and our issuance of new shares to the venture capitalists, our stock now has a value of $2 a share. You can each do the arithmetic for your respective options. As they say in the options business, you are all now **above water**. In other words, the price of the stock is above what you would pay if you exercised your options. In fact, I'd say you're well above water." Johnny thinks about trying to explain the distinction between common and preferred shares, but decides that that would just complicate things unnecessarily.

Jeff isn't done, though. "What if we wanted to sell some of our stock and go out and buy a nice new car?"

Now Johnny is frowning slightly, holding his chin. "Well, you couldn't do that, yet. First off, you're not **vested**. You have to hold your options for a year before you can begin exercising them to acquire stock. Even if you were vested, it probably wouldn't pay for you to exercise options at this point. That's because the company is **privately held**. There are just a few of us—the outside directors, the venture capitalists and I—who actually own stock. You really wouldn't be able to sell your stock until we have an initial public offering, or IPO, and the stock becomes **publicly held**. Or unless the company is acquired by another company. Then there would be a market for your stock."

As the employees file out of the room, Johnny calls to Jeff to remain behind for a few minutes. "Jeff, you remember when you joined the company, I asked you if you wanted to get rich, and you said you did. You've been a big part of our success, and I want to follow through on that commitment. So I'm going to make some additional options available to you. Only now, because the venture capitalists have valued us so highly, our common stock has a **strike price** of 50 cents a share, so our board of directors has set the exercise price at that same amount. The valuation has to do with preferred stock, which is held by the venture capitalists, and common stock, which is the stock you get by exercising your options, but I'm not going to get into all that, since it gets pretty conceptual. In any event, I'm going to provide you with an additional 20,000 options at 50 cents a share. I expect the stock to continue on up from here."

The Fun Begins
Nine months later

Again it's late on a Thursday afternoon. Johnny has convened another company meeting. Only this time, the meeting is being held in Superfastgrowth.com's "fun room"—an expansive conference room with a small pool table to one side, beach balls scattered about, a cappuccino machine in one corner, and a tiny artificial-turf putting green in another corner.

"This is the day we've all been anticipating," Johnny tells the 40 people crowding the room. "We've just filed a **registration statement** with the **Securities and Exchange Commission**, the federal agency that oversees public

46

companies. If all goes according to plan, we'll have our IPO within two months. The **underwriters,** the Wall Street people who put these things together, tell us that our stock could come out at $10 a share. Nobody knows exactly what it will do after that. But you've all seen what's happened to some offerings, how the shares have skyrocketed. I don't want to make any promises, but that could happen here."

The next afternoon

Johnny calls Jeff into his expansive office.

"Well, Jeff, it's been quite a ride, huh?"

"It sure has, Johnny. It's hard to believe it's only been a little over a year, given all that's happened."

"Jeff, you're one of the reasons we're here," Johnny says. "It looks like you should make out really well on those original options on 75,000 shares, and you won't do badly on those additional 20,000 options."

"Well, that brings up a question I have," says Jeff. "I understand about the vesting. But I have a friend who also works at an Internet company that went public a few months ago, and that company had a provision in its stock option plan that provided for **immediate vesting** if the firm went public or was sold. Do we have that?"

Johnny fidgets. "Well, no, we don't. My thinking when we set up the plan was that even if we went public or sold the company, we'd want people to have incentives to keep everyone working hard. But you know, Jeff, because you've been with Superfastgrowth.com for just over a year, you'll be able to buy one-fourth of your initial 75,000 options, which is something in the neighborhood of 18,000-plus shares, right away. That could be worth a cool $180,000, or even more if the stock heads up. If you do sell your stock, think of me and the **lockup period** I'm subject to on my founders stock. I have to hold my stock for at least six months before selling the shares. That's something our underwriters insisted on, since they don't want all the insiders selling their stock at the same time, and possibly depressing the stock. Just keep in mind that if you do sell your shares right away, you'll be subject to some pretty high taxes, as if you received additional salary and got put into a higher tax bracket, so you could be looking at federal and state income taxes of about 40% on your gain. If you hold the stock for at least a year, you'll be subject to the capital gains tax, which is a maximum of 20% in federal taxes, and perhaps a few percent more in state taxes."

Jeff is still irritated. "I'm not pleased about the vesting. We all worked our butts off for this moment, and we should be able to cash in all our chips."

Johnny ignores the criticism. "There is some additional good news here, Jeff. I want to reward you and a few other people who have worked so hard with some additional options. So, I'm granting you options on another 10,000 shares. You'll be able to exercise them at $10 a share. Even though it's not nearly as good a deal as when you joined, it could turn out to be a very good deal if the stock does as well as I think it could. I'm limited in the exercise price I can offer now because the value of the company has gone up so much."

"Great," says Jeff. "But when do I actually get all my *cash*? I just seem to continually get new pieces of paper."

"Be patient, Jeff. Be patient."

Real-World Concerns
Six months later

The IPO is an exciting event, especially during the first two months, as the stock heads steadily higher. After the first month, the stock is at $20 a share, and after the second month it has edged up to $25 a share. Employees monitor the price nearly continuously during the day, and anytime there is a significant movement up or down, there's a comment from one or another cubby, "Looks like we're up a point," or "We've taken a bit of a tumble."

During the third month, though, the stock begins falling, at first just a quarter or half a point on a typical day, but then sometimes by a point or two. It closes the month at $18 a share. By the end of the fourth month, it is down to $9 a share, and some of the newer employees, who had received options just as the IPO was being filed, at $10 a share, complain of being **under water**.

The employees now monitor the stock much less frequently, and when it goes down, which is more days than it goes up, there is usually little comment. By the end of the fifth month, when the stock is down to $6 a share, a few employees begin sending their resumes out to other companies to change jobs. Jeff is one of them. Nor is he dissuaded when Superfastgrowth.com institutes a **stock purchase plan** whereby employees can buy small amounts of stock—typically a few hundred shares—at a discount of 15% off the average price of the preceding three months. The problem with the plan is that every time anyone buys stock, it seems to go down way more than 15%.

Old Paper
Eight months later

Jeff has been with Superfastgrowth.com for a little over three years at this point. Two months earlier, with the stock at $5 a share, Jeff sold his initial 18,000-plus shares, pocketing a little over $90,000. Jeff felt like kicking himself—by holding the stock for one year, he qualified for the lower capital gains rate, but he was selling the stock at one-fifth of its high. On the advice of his accountant, he immediately places $18,000 into a savings account, to be sure he'll have the 20% capital gains tax he expects to owe.

Jeff also makes one more decision: He decides to depart Superfastgrowth.com and take a job with a new

Internet startup. At the time he leaves, the company's stock is $4 a share. Jeff decides to take two additional "mopping-up" steps.

First, he exercises the second and third one-fourths of his original options at 10 cents a share and, after paying the $3,600 purchase price, immediately sells the shares for $144,000 (36,000 shares times $4 a share). Sure, he'll have to pay taxes at the higher income rate on his $140,400 gain (the difference between $144,000 and $3,600), but at least he'll have something.

Second, 59 days after leaving Superfastgrowth.com, with his vested options due to **expire** the next day, he exercises the first one-fourth of the later 20,000 options he is now eligible to buy at 50 cents a share for $2,500 (5,000 shares at 50 cents a share). He immediately sells the shares for $4 a share as well, for $20,000, or a gain of $17,500. He thinks briefly about holding those shares longer, but concludes that the key to rejuvenating Superfastgrowth.com is to replace Johnny as president, but Johnny shows no intention of leaving.

When Jeff leave Superfastgrowth.com, he **forfeits** the remaining one-fourth of his options on the original 75,000 shares, and three-fourths of the options he was entitled to on the later option grant of 20,000 shares, and all of the 10,000 shares.

Six years later

Jeff is cleaning out some old files, and comes across his Superfastgrowth.com file. There, he finds his original option agreement. He does an online search and discovers that Superfastgrowth.com is still in existence, trading at $3 a share. It's held steady at about that price for a year.

As Jeff puts away the old files, he shakes his head in amazement. He's worked for three Internet startup companies, including Superfastgrowth.com, over the last nine years. And each has turned out pretty much like the other—some modest gains, but no big hits of the type achieved by the Microsoft Millionaires. What's he been doing wrong? For whatever reason, he's been unable to pick the super winners, he realizes. He's not sure why, but he just hasn't.

Jeff's problem is that he's been making his job/investment decisions based on the wrong criteria. What does he need to do to correct the problem? He needs to assess his own tolerance for risk and take more care evaluating prospective employers. In other words, he needs to stop listening to people like Johnny Sweetalker and focus on the real issues associated with obtaining stock options that will achieve his expectations. More on those issues ahead. ■

Chapter 5

What Kind of Employee Investor Are You?

What is your comfort level with financial and career risk? Your answer to this question will go a long way toward determining your ability to take advantage of stock option opportunities. The more comfortable you are with financial and career risk, the likelier you'll be to act on an attractive stock option situation. You just need to always recognize the key distinction between investing money in the stock market, and investing yourself into a stock option situation.

sk any knowledgeable investment expert how best to develop an investment strategy, and you'll invariably hear a variation on this statement: "First and foremost, you need to decide the level of risk you can tolerate."

So it should be with you as you evaluate potential jobs or contracts that include equity. In deciding whether to invest your time and expertise in a venture, you need to begin by determining your own tolerance for risk. Once you do that, the rest of the decision-making process becomes fairly analytical. But determining your risk-tolerance level is a highly personal evaluation that only you can complete.

You must determine the answers to the following questions:

53

1. How comfortable are you investing significantly in equity (stock)?
2. How comfortable are you taking risks with your career?
3. How well can you match your investment and career aspirations?
4. What kind of financial and career investor are you?

This chapter examines these questions in more detail, and provides guidance for handling stock option situations based on your answers.

Are You Excited or Scared By Equity?

It's easy to be intimidated by the terminology surrounding investing—terms like equity, options, warrants, short selling, debentures, bonds, etc. Most fundamentally, there are only two types of investments, broadly speaking: equity and debt.

Equity consists of a stake you hold in a company (or any other entity, such as your house). You invest in a company and you receive some amount of stock, expressed as shares, in the company. Yes, there are things like options, warrants, and short selling, but those things are all part and parcel of the investment process.

Debt consists of loans. When you buy U.S. Treasury Notes or corporate bonds, you are loaning money. In the case of the Treasury Notes, you are loaning money to the U.S. government. In the case of corporate bonds that you buy when they are issued, you are loaning money to the corporation issuing the bonds.

Equity is generally considered riskier than loans, since there is no legal obligation for repayment of equity investors. Surveys of the American public have shown an increasing percentage of Americans willing to make equity investments, thanks to the rising stock market, but even so, only about half of Americans have money in stocks.

Two examples from my experiences hiring employees at the Internet services company I cofounded help illustrate the different views people have of equity:

Back in late 1995, when the company was seeking its first employee, my partner and I interviewed a 35-year-old part-time business school student who was contemplating a career shift into technology sales from home construction. Such a shift wasn't as radical as it might seem, since the man, Josh, had graduated from an Ivy League college and was so obviously bright, creative, and motivated.

As we talked with Josh for more than an hour about his goals and ambitions, and it became clear that he could be a real find for us, I decided that the time had come to be frank and open with him. "Josh, we really like what you have to offer. But I have to be honest with you. This is a startup company, and we can't afford to pay you very much—certainly nothing approaching market rates. But we can offer you an opportunity to learn about the latest Internet technology, as well as to share in the growth of this venture."

Josh didn't have to be prompted more than once. "That's why I'm here, because it is a startup," he said. "I'm interested in the stock options that are going to make me a lot of money."

We hired Josh at a salary not much above minimum wage and he became the creator of Internet tools that helped the company grow into a serious online direct marketing agency. As the company expanded, his interest in stock options continued unabated. Whenever Josh had a salary review, he requested that he be given additional options in exchange for somewhat smaller salary increases than he might otherwise have received. After four years with the company, when it had grown to more than 15 employees, Josh was the third-largest shareholder after the two founders.

Contrast Josh's approach with that of a man I'll call Richard, a 40-year-old computer programmer I helped interview two years after Josh joined our company, when we stood at about a half dozen employees. Richard had previously worked with us on a contract basis, helping on some programming projects. Josh liked his work, and now wanted to expand Richard's responsibilities. However, Richard's hourly rates were burdensome to us, so we decided to try to convince him to lower his hourly rates, or even come to work with us as an employee, in exchange for stock options.

Richard's "day job" was as a programmer with a nonprofit organization. He said he was open to potentially changing positions, and pointed out that several of his techie friends had taken jobs with technology firms that provided stock options that had risen significantly in value.

Most of our one-and-a-half-hour interview focused on questions he had about stock options. Would he get to vote his shares? Would he receive dividends if the company showed a profit? Would he have to pay in if the company had a loss? If he left the company shortly after acquiring stock, was there a way for him to sell it? What if we changed the name of the company, and maintained the old company, in which he was a shareholder, as a shell?

I tried to explain to Richard that options weren't the same as stock, and that he wouldn't actually own anything until he exercised the options. But each answer seemed to trigger three more questions. I realized after a while that some of Richard's concerns stemmed from naiveté. I finally told him, "You're just going to have to trust us on a lot of this."

After a few days, Richard informed us that he wasn't interested in lowering his hourly rate and taking stock options for part of his compensation, nor did he want to take a full-time job with us. He preferred his existing

56

arrangement—working for us evenings and weekends and being compensated entirely in cash based on his existing hourly cash rate.

While I never got into a conversation with Richard about his investment philosophy, I would guess that he probably kept most of his savings in bank accounts or money market accounts and avoided equity investments entirely.

Are You Excited or Scared By Career Risk?

The real issue for both Josh and Richard was risk. Josh was comfortable with considerable investment risk. Richard was uncomfortable with much investment risk.

And if you consider the second question posed at the start of this chapter—about your comfort level taking risks with your career—the relationship to the first question begins to become clearer. Josh was not only comfortable with much investment risk, he was also quite comfortable with a great deal of career risk, ready to abandon his well-established contracting business for the great unknown of the Internet. Richard was nervous about receiving stock in place of cash and also wanted to avoid risking his secure job for one with an Internet company.

All of which begins to make the point that your comfort with career and investment risk are likely to be related. If you are most attracted to a job in a large, stable organization with lots of benefits, then you are likely not going to be attracted to investing your spare cash in young technology companies. Similarly, if you are most interested in working for an early-stage Internet company, you are probably going to be more comfortable investing in speculative technology companies.

All that being said, the issue of your job as an investment isn't simply a matter of determining your comfort level with varying amounts of risk. Your job is usually something for which you have trained based on your interests and aptitudes. It is where you spend the largest single segment of your time. If you enjoy your job, the time moves much more quickly than if you don't.

Whether or not you enjoy your job is related to all kinds of things, like the actual tasks you do, the amount of responsibility you have, what your boss is like, how you interact with coworkers, and the opportunities you have for advancement, not to mention your compensation and benefits. But there is something else involved, as well: your commitment to the organization for which you are working. Most of us like to feel good about the company in which we are investing our time—because of the quality of its products or services, and/or because of its potential for growing quickly and becoming a major force in its industry.

The matter of career risk can come up in a number of ways. But usually it is related to a new opportunity of some sort. If you are asked to take a new position within your existing organization, perhaps in a different group or division, the opportunity is laden with some risk. If you have an opportunity for a new position within an entirely different organization, the risk is likely even greater. And if you decide to leave an existing position without having secured a new position, the risk is likely to be greater still.

What Comes First, the Investment or the Job?

The whole area of jobs and careers is one that I have intentionally avoided exploring too deeply, simply because there are so many excellent books about the subject already available. It is possible to examine the matter from dozens of angles associated with your preferences, skills, and the existing marketplace.

The aspect of careers that tends not to be examined very closely is that pertaining to the third question I raised at the start of this chapter—the linkage between careers and investment. The emergence of equity incentives in the job market has made this linkage more important than ever now that a decision one way or the other can mean a difference between hundreds of thousands and perhaps even millions of dollars in compensation over just a few years.

The linkage between career and investing isn't something that every individual can fully control. Chances are that if you most enjoy teaching second grade—because you like working with young children and being in an elementary school environment—you aren't going to find as many opportunities for a job that offers stock options or other equity opportunities as you will if you are a computer programmer specializing in Java or ColdFusion.

This isn't to say that if you are a teacher or a social worker that the opportunity to earn options is closed off to you. It just means you'll have to be more imaginative in your job hunting. For example, a number of educators have found jobs with equity opportunities in some of the many education-related software and Internet companies that have sprung up in recent years. A former English teacher hired in late 1999 by the company I cofounded discovered a surprise bonus in cash and stock from her options when the company was sold a month after she signed on. Needless to say, she grew very quickly to adore the idea of stock options.

Generally speaking, the matter of equity becomes more of a variable in two types of situations:

1. Your job interests and desires can be satisfied in any of several jobs. For example, you can be a Web site designer in a startup company or in a large corporation.

2. You have made a conscious decision to obtain a job—any job—in an "equity-promising" situation. In other words, you don't care what you do, you just want to work in a company where you're likeliest to obtain the maximum amount of stock with the highest potential valuation in the shortest period of time.

You have the most analysis to do if you're in the first situation, since you must consider job issues as well as company issues. If you are in the second situation, your concerns will be more limited, focused primarily on company issues.

What's Your Investment "Philosophy"?

Private investors—venture capitalists and so-called "angel" investors—can generally be divided into two broad groups:

1. Active investors. These are investors who don't just want to invest money. They want to provide their expertise, as well, to the entrepreneurs they back. Active entrepreneurs—those who understand the vagaries of fast-changing marketplaces—usually want to be involved with active investors.

2. Passive investors. These are investors who write out an investment check and walk away. They may sound like ideal investors—you receive your cash and you're on your own. But in reality, such investors can present the most difficulties for an entrepreneur because they can't fully appreciate the scope of the challenges the business faces. So when they call in once a month . . . once a week . . . or several times a day for information on how their investment is doing, providing explanations can be nearly impossible.

The world of employee investors can be similarly divided. People like Josh are active investors. They want to do well. But they also want to be integral to growing the company, in terms of their skills and commitment. Because they understand how their skills fit into the overall needs of the company, they can ask intelligent questions about company issues as a whole, and understand what they're being told. Josh is a technical person, but he has questions about marketing and promotion of the company's technology. Even if he doesn't always agree with the

60

company's marketing and promotion tactics, he usually understands the logic behind the tactics, as well as the fact that he doesn't have expertise in these areas.

Increasingly, "cash investors" have begun popping up in high-tech companies, especially Internet-related companies, in search of stock options. These are individuals more in search of quick and substantial investment profits from stock options and less committed to a particular company and culture.

Major media have taken to writing about such individuals, much the way they write about lottery winners and gamblers. *The Wall Street Journal* in its August 10, 1998, issue profiled two young women who were best friends and migrated among the accounting departments of Silicon Valley companies they judged to be good candidates for stock appreciation. The two, Cheri Kalenian and Sheila Leary, worked at four technology and Internet companies between 1991 and 1998, collecting options at each stop. At one company, Remedy Corp., Kalenian says she made 80 times her money. At OnSale Inc., an Internet auction company, the value of her options soared as the company's stock tripled in price during her first eight months there.

The New York Times in its Dec. 23, 1999, issue described Amaryllis Diaz, a 28-year-old New Yorker who left a customer service job she had held for years with an industrial printer to become a supervisor in the customer service department of GiftCertificates.com. A key motivation? Not the salary of something under $40,000, but the stock options that she said could provide "a nice bonus."

Inc. magazine in its February 1998 edition recounted the story of Frank Lee, a manager who hopped around Silicon Valley companies—from Synoptics, a networking company, to 3-Com, to a technology startup. At Synoptics, he had options that soared in value as the stock went from $12 a share when he joined to $120 a share within two years.

Figuring he had fully exploited that run, he went to 3Com, where on his first day the company announced a stock split, doubling the number of shares to which he had access to options. Following a short stint at 3Com, he headed off to an Internet startup.

Such individuals have decided that the investment component of their jobs outweighs the career component. By taking jobs that often pay less than what they might make were it not for the stock options, these individuals use the excess value as an investment, hoping to gain a big score that more than compensates for the reduced pay.

The Risk-Reward Rule

Regardless of whether you are an Active Investor or a Passive Investor, you want your options to pay the largest possible returns. As noted at the start of this chapter, developing an investment strategy begins with an assessment of how much risk you are prepared to take.

Generally speaking in investing, the greater the risk, the greater the potential reward. What that means in practical terms is that the earlier you invest in the next Microsoft or Dell Computer—before the investment has been anointed the next Microsoft or Dell—the more money you'll make. Of course, the earlier you invest in such a situation, the greater the risk you will be taking, since the earlier you invest, the less obvious it will be that the venture can achieve such lofty heights.

The same dynamics apply to your assessment of a potential employer. The earlier in a company's life you take a job, generally speaking, the greater is the risk that the company won't succeed. But if the company does succeed, those who were there at the earliest points are the ones who reap the largest rewards. Those who arrive later, when the outcome is clearer, receive lower rewards. Even a few months can make a significant difference, as Sheri Kalenian and Sheila Leary, the close friends described in *The Wall Street Journal* article noted previously, discovered. Kalenian joined Remedy Corp. in 1994, just prior to its going public. Leary followed Kalenian there in 1995, after its stock flattened out from its initial pop. So, while Kalenian made 80 times the money she invested to buy shares from her options and other stock purchases, Leary struck out on her options for 1,500 shares.

There are important exceptions to this tendency, though. Increasingly, quite young companies—less than six months old—are obtaining multimillion-dollar venture capital investments. A three-month-old company with $25 million of venture capital in the bank represents a much smaller risk from a survivability perspective than a ten-year-old company that has been losing market share and recording operating losses for the previous three years, and has only enough cash to carry it through another month.

Later chapters provide you with guidance for determining a company's exact financial status. But let's assume for now that my original statement holds true—that the earlier in a company's life you get involved, the greater the risk. That helps explain why the founding entrepreneurs—the individuals who come up with the business concept and quit their jobs to turn it into reality—wind up with the largest chunks of stock ownership.

But there is much more to investing successfully in a job than being there early. You need to be there with the right stuff. And you need to be able to assess at a very early stage whether one situation is more attractive than another. Being there with the right approach is the subject of the next chapter, and effectively assessing whether you want to take the job is the focus of the chapter after that. ■

63

Chapter 6

Equity Sweet Spots—Match Yourself with the Right Situation

Timing is everything when it comes to cashing in on stock options. Get in too early, and your patience may be tested. Get in after an IPO or acquisition, and you may strike out on the really big gains. When are the best times to get in, the "sweet spots"? Learn about four sweet spots here. Moreover, you need to determine if you have what it takes to be an "option type employee" who will be showered with stock option opportunities.

The key to making money via equity incentives is much the same as succeeding in other areas of life—being in the right place at the right time with the right stuff.

Sure, luck is part of the game. But it's really a much smaller part than we might like to think. In the game of equity incentives, you can do a lot to make your own luck—much more than you might think.

How do you get yourself into the right place at the right time with the right stuff? Perhaps more important, how do you recognize when everything is "right"?

65

In this chapter, I begin the process of explaining how you evaluate venture situations to determine the likelihood of their equity increasing in value. The process is actually similar to what professional investors go through in evaluating companies they are considering for investment. Except there's a twist you need to handle that's different from the investors—as explained in Chapter 2, your investment is in the form of your time and energy rather than your money.

Part of what you're trying to avoid is being swept off your feet by a Johnny Sweetalker (memorialized in Chapter 4). Not that you don't want to work for a Johnny Sweetalker. It's just that you want your decision to do so to be influenced by information you obtain and analysis you conduct apart from what such an individual is likely to provide.

To help you begin the evaluation process, I pose a number of key questions you need to consider as you assess your opportunities for obtaining equity.

What Are You Really Trying to Accomplish?

Sure, I know you're trying to get rich. But more to the point, you are trying to accomplish two other things:

1. You're trying to gain ownership in a company that is going to be worth lots of money in the not-too-distant future.

2. You're trying to gain ownership in a company whose stock you can sell and convert into cash in the not-too-distant future, sometimes referred to as gaining *liquidity*.

Achieving one of these goals without the other won't get you rich. Gaining options to purchase stock in a company that's already public provides liquidity, but that liquidity means nothing if the stock goes down because the company has been mismanaged. And obtaining stock in a fast-growing private company controlled by an individual who has no intention of making the stock easily sellable in the not-too-distant future will likely frustrate you—"water, water everywhere, but not a drop to drink," in the words of Ahab in the classic, *Moby Dick.*

When my partner and I were trying to sell our online direct marketing agency, we negotiated seriously with a larger, privately-held direct marketing agency that was seeking an Internet presence. The owner was quite interested in investing in our company to grow it and further increase its value. But when we inquired about his plans for a "liquidity event," such as an initial public offering or a sale of his company, he hesitated. No, he was only in his late thirties and he loved what he was doing. He wanted to continue growing his company together with any acquisitions he made, and really had no plans for giving up ownership control anytime in the near future.

The bottom line for my partner and me, along with our employee option holders, was that while we'd all have ownership in a company with likely a great deal of value, we'd have no way to turn that value into cash anytime soon because we would be giving up control to someone who didn't have that as a priority. So we eventually passed on that deal.

Of course, if a company is already publicly held, then the question of liquidity doesn't apply, since its stock is liquid. The key question for such a company is how well its stock will appreciate over the coming one to three years. If a company is publicly held, its financial and other operating information is publicly available (more on checking companies out in Chapter 10).

As you go through the process of evaluating companies with which to be involved, you'll discover that most companies fail to pass muster on both these questions. And remember, these are just your very initial screening criteria.

Where Do You Find Candidate Companies?

In a broad sense, finding companies likeliest to make you rich is like finding a needle in a haystack. As noted, the math is against you. More than one million new businesses are started each year. Yet, fewer than one thousand of these wind up going public. And of those that go public, perhaps a few hundred will post attractive gains a year or two after the IPO, and an even smaller number of those will be long-term growth companies with ongoing stock market gains.

But this isn't to say that you can't gain a foothold in a company that has the potential to achieve at least modest gains that will pay you a significant bonus sometime in the near-term future. Recent surveys suggest that many more companies are making stock options available to employees than did so even seven or eight years ago. The National Center for Employee Ownership estimated in 1999 that employee control of American equity had more than quadrupled from less than 2% at the end of the 1980s to more than 8% at the end of the 1990s. A late-1990s survey of one thousand publicly-held companies by ShareData, a provider of software and services to companies providing options, found that three-fourths of companies it sampled with less than $50 million of annual sales and two-thirds of those with fewer than one hundred employees offered option plans to all employees.

So finding companies willing to talk about options has gotten easier, which increases your odds of finding attractive situations. There are ways to begin honing in on companies with the right stuff. The critical initial criteria include the following:

■ *You need to be in the right location.* This means being close to centers of entrepreneurial activity. Simply put, you're much more likely to find a company with attractive equity prospects in Palo Alto, CA, than you are in Sioux Falls, SD. Palo Alto, of course, is in the heart of Silicon

Valley, an entrepreneurial hotbed where dozens of promising new companies seem to start up each week.

That doesn't mean you need to pack up and move to Palo Alto, however. Fortunately, there are an increasing number of areas with opportunities similar to those offered in Palo Alto and the rest of Silicon Valley. Areas with a large number of fast-growing companies include Boston, Seattle, New York City, Dallas, Austin (TX), Las Vegas, and Denver. And as the Internet makes location less important for the operation of many companies, we are seeing promising companies spring up in ever-less-likely places like Cape Cod and Wyoming.

■ *You need to be plugged into the right industries.* Increasingly, this means being involved with technology and Internet companies. If you look at the industries that have performed best as measured by the stock markets, then high technology and related Internet companies have been the place to be.

That's not to say you need to be a computer geek to have any hope of making money on equity incentives. Individuals who are able to transfer their skills from one industry to another can do very well. For example, a fair number of writers and editors have made money via equity incentives by moving from traditional magazines and newspapers to online publishing ventures. At the company I cofounded, we hired several writers who had no previous Internet experience; they received stock options that turned into significant amounts of cash when the company was sold in late 1999.

Technology companies need bookkeepers, project managers, human resource experts, and other types of "non techie" employees. Of course, it helps if you either know something about technology or have had some prior experience in the technology world, so you can talk the lingo. Knowing something about technology often means educating yourself about computers and reading trade publications that explain the issues at work in particular areas of the technology arena.

In addition, various nontechnology industries are sprouting very attractive companies that are leveraging the Internet to become successful. Book retailer Barnes & Noble set up Barnesandnoble.com. As I noted earlier, *Inc.* magazine established Inc.com as a separate venture. All varieties of manufacturers, distributors, and referral services that help bring buyers and sellers together are springing up, as well.

You also need to be prepared to go out and find the promising companies. This means logging onto the career sites where promising companies search out people, like Monster.com and CareerCity.com. Increasing numbers of companies make it known in their online want ads that they offer "equity incentives" or "stock option programs." It also means getting involved with professional associations and other groups whose members are likely to be plugged into interesting situations, as well as staying in touch with friends and associates working in the business world—in other words, networking.

If you are a professional, then you may be able to plug into the network of professional recruiters, sometimes referred to as "headhunters," that operates in large cities around the country. Because many of them are in regular contact with fast-growing companies that offer equity incentives, they can help lead you to significant opportunities. Just be aware that they are paid by employers after an individual is hired, so they may try to push you into situations that don't necessarily represent the best career or financial opportunities.

■ *You need points of comparison.* It's important to evaluate more than one potential company candidate so as to get a feel for what the marketplace has to offer. The idea is to be able to compare not only job offers, but the potential valuations of companies you are considering. Working with headhunters can help in quickly providing points of comparison. Ideally, you'll have several opportunities so that you can make an informed choice.

What Are the Equity Sweet Spots?

As you examine potential employers that seem to be saying the right things with regard to their growth prospects and liquidity orientation, and are willing to make options available, you should be thinking about timing, as in: When will any options I am granted be likeliest to have significant value?

The situations for which you should most be on the lookout are those that provide a valuation to stock that previously hasn't been fairly valued. These include:

■ *An initial public offering (IPO).* In terms of valuation increases, this is usually the premier event. A lawyer I know well who long specialized in handling small-company initial public offerings (IPOs) once said to me: "You get the best valuations from a public offering because the general public is much less sophisticated than professional investors." During 1999, IPOs showed an average of 60% gains during their first day of trading, while during the first couple of months of 2000, the first-day gains were about 100%, according to *The New York Times* of March 19, 2000.

■ *An acquisition.* Generally speaking, an acquisition is the second-most desirable event to occur. In its best form, a publicly-held company acquires the organization in which you hold options for a combination of cash and stock. That way, you get some initial cash, plus an opportunity to see additional gains from the new stock you obtain. This is what happened in the case of the Internet company I cofounded,

71

which was acquired by a larger company for a combination of cash and stock.

■ *Private investment.* While this usually isn't a liquidity event for the shareholders, it often precedes one by a relatively short time span—say one to three years. It also has the advantage of attaching a value to the shares on which you have options. If you have options available at 10 cents a share, and venture capitalists invest at a valuation of $1.00 a share, you know your shares already have achieved a ten-fold increase in value—on paper, at least. If things continue to go well, an IPO or acquisition will occur with an even higher valuation.

■ *A sharp dip in stock markets.* Remember, the idea here is to get options at low prices, and eventually sell the stock at high prices. If you are taking a job with a publicly-held company, the best time to sign on is when the company's stock is very low, because the options you receive will be exercisable at the low price. Even if you are already working for a publicly-held company, a sharp dip in its stock price could be a good time to seek out a raise—in the form of additional stock options. Another approach is to convince your employer to reprice your options, but this is usually a more difficult task since repricing options downward requires companies to make an accounting adjustment that can adversely affect profits. An excellent time for many employees to seek out additional options occurred during the spring of 2000, when the NASDAQ market plummeted during March and April. And a number of companies repriced employees' options downward in the interests of retaining valued people.

It's easy to make a wrong decision in this arena, however, even when an opportunity is seemingly staring you in the face. The Jan. 4, 2000, *Wall Street Journal* recounted the story of a sales executive at iVillage Inc., an Internet startup catering to women, who received options on 280,000 shares in the young company at $1.60 a share. The shares were supposed to vest over four years, beginning after a year on the job. The executive was fired after nine months, in the spring of 1999, but was allowed to purchase the first one-fourth of his option shares, or 70,000 shares. That meant he had to come up with about $100,000 within a few weeks, before the options expired.

The executive knew that an IPO was imminent, but he didn't have the $100,000 handy. Why didn't he just borrow it? According to the newspaper, he wasn't sure the IPO would be successful, and even if it were, he would have to wait six months (his lockup period) before being able to sell his shares, by which time the shares could have lost much of their value. So he let the options expire.

Sure enough, iVillage went public at $24 a share, which would have made his shares worth $1.7 million. Even six months later, the shares were worth close to that same amount. Not a good move by the executive.

The New Realities of Equity Sweet Spots

Conventional wisdom has it that the best point in time to become associated with, and obtain options from, a fast-growing company is some months prior to an IPO. The want-ad I quoted from at the start of Chapter 3 played on that idea. The thinking is that the company's common shares will be valued much lower than the initial public offering price. And for many years, this was true. You might join a small company, receive options at an exercise price of $2 a share, and then six months or a year later see your company go public at $15 a share, with the price doubling or tripling within a day or two.

Over the last couple of years, though, this conventional wisdom has changed. Because so many companies have been going public so early in their life cycles—sometimes just a year or two after formation—the federal Securities and Exchange Commission (SEC), which oversees public companies for the government, has been urging companies to keep their stock option exercise prices in line with reality. So increasingly, the boards of directors of fast-growing private companies on a path to go public are increasing their companies' exercise prices more often and more sharply than ever before.

The effect for individuals who join companies that are close to completing public offerings is to receive stock options at an exercise price that isn't far below the price at which the company actually goes public.

■ *A more interesting approach.* With small companies "growing up" so quickly, here's another way to play the equity sweet spot game:

Instead of seeking out companies about to go public, look for companies that have within the last few months received a significant ($10 million-plus) round of private investor financing. The fact that they have received financing tells you that savvy investors see promise in the companies. It also tells you that the companies have cash to meet their expenses for some months looking ahead. And perhaps most significantly from a stock options viewpoint, it tells you that an initial public offering is likely not imminent.

In this situation, you'll be joining the company at a time when the investors' preferred shares are valued much more highly than the common shares available for purchase via stock option plans. (See Chapter 4 for a more detailed explanation about the difference between preferred and common stock as affects stock options.) Thus, you're getting the benefit of a certain amount of security (endorsement and cash from investors) along with a wide price disparity between preferred and common stock. You'll find more information on researching these situations in Chapter 10.

How Attractive Are You as an "Option Employee"?

You can do all kinds of investigating and analysis, but if your chosen company isn't willing to extend you an offer, then it's all for naught.

Moreover, once you get an offer, you want to be sure you maximize the amount of equity you receive. You don't want to sign on for options on 10,000 shares when you could have obtained options on 20,000 shares just by negotiating harder.

The key here is convincing your chosen company of two things:

1. *That you are an "option type employee."* Remember, you are an "investor," providing skills, creativity, experience, and commitment rather than money. Part of your challenge is convincing your targeted companies that you have all these attributes in spades, because these are the attributes they are seeking. They want to know that the options they provide will indeed motivate you. The companies that offer the most obviously attractive stock options are often the toughest ones to gain attention from because the competition is so intense. Microsoft has been one such company, subjecting applicants to grueling interviews and assessments in its effort to hire the smartest, most talented people available. Another more recent example of a high-flyer with high barriers to entry is Amazon.com. According to a May 4, 1999, article in *The Wall Street Journal* about Amazon.com's hiring practices, "A company like this needs the right staff to achieve its lofty goals, but getting in the door isn't easy. Chief Executive Jeff Bezos wants stars on his staff, not the merely competent."

2. *That it needs you in the worst way.* Your goal is to maximize the "salivation factor." Because the most promising companies are growing quickly, they nearly always have "people holes" to fill. Depending on how dire their need to fill a particular hole is, and how attractive you look, you'll get them salivating.

I was on the salivating end in the spring of 1999, shortly after our agency's project director resigned quite suddenly. This was a key position in the company that we couldn't replace immediately because there were few people with the combination of editorial, Internet, and management experience we required. Fortunately for the company, I was able to take over and handle the position temporarily. But we knew we needed to fill it, and quickly. We concluded after a few weeks that the only way we would fill it was to raid a similar company for the right person. We found a candidate, an assistant project director, at another Internet company, and determined that she wanted to step up to a position of greater responsibility. Moreover, she told us she had felt let down when the company she was working for was acquired by a larger company, because she didn't have any options.

After a couple of interviews with Gloria, we decided she would make a great project director, and that we were determined to hire her at all costs. She had us salivating. "Have we got a deal for you," we said to her, essentially. We offered her options on more shares than we had ever offered a new employee, plus a substantial hike from her previous salary. She accepted, and we filled our hole.

Putting It All Together

The decision making around these matters—which job to take, how many options you should receive, whether a candidate company is really poised to make it big—can be very tricky. Subsequent chapters further explore various aspects of the analysis you should complete.

You may be wondering at this point about proper form. Do you investigate first to choose candidate companies or do you go after interesting job prospects first and then investigate? There is no easy answer to this question.

My advice is to do both. If you read about an interesting company in the local paper that you think might need your skills, you may want to investigate further—look at its Web site, check out other articles about the company—and then apply. Yet, there's no reason you shouldn't be willing to explore a particularly attractive job opportunity without first knowing a great deal about the company. With the knowledge you are gaining from this book, you will be able to determine more quickly than otherwise whether you want to continue with the job application process for a particular company. ■

Chapter 7

How Much Is Your Potential Employer Worth?

To focus in on what your stock options are likely worth, you have to know what your employer company is worth. Amazing as it may sound, you need not be an accountant to begin figuring a company's valuation. You do need to do some detective work during and after your job interviews, though. What questions do you ask during an interview? Whom do you call inside and outside the company? Where can you find published information on a privately-held company? If you wait for an offer to come first, it may be too late to arm yourself for the negotiating table.

T he title of this chapter may well provoke two questions: Why should I care what my employer is worth? And even if I should care, who the hell am I to be valuing a company?

These are perfectly logical questions. Placing a financial value on prospective employers isn't something many job-search books advise. And if they did, wouldn't such a task be way beyond the abilities of a novice? After all, there are professional accountants and financial experts who train for years to become adept at valuing companies.

The reason you should care is that company valuation is the key issue from which most everything else about the value of stock options and other equity incentives flows.

79

Most basically, once you have a realistic company valuation, you can calculate the value of shares outstanding. For example, if a company can reasonably be considered to be worth $5 million and it has one million shares outstanding, then its stock would be worth $5 a share.

Once you know that, you can begin to ascribe a value to options that may be offered to you. If you are offered options on 10,000 shares of a company at $1 a share and you have good reason to feel that the company is worth $5 a share, then you have a basis for ascribing the options' compensation value to you at $40,000 ($50,000 value minus the $10,000 cost to you). This is essentially a more reality-based version of the exercise that Johnny Sweetalker went through in Chapter 4. (For the purposes of illustration, I have assumed that this hypothetical company has only common shares outstanding; if it also has preferred stock, then the computation becomes more complex, as described in Chapter 4, but the underlying issue of valuation is the same.)

The key challenge, of course, is arriving at that $5 million valuation. Or rather, coming up with that valuation (or any valuation) and feeling confident that it has a real-world basis.

While you may not be able to come up with precise valuations, the reality is that you as a novice can make informed judgments about the valuations being attached to prospective employers, or even come up with your own valuation range that won't be laughed at by professionals. This chapter and the next two provide background and guidance that can help you make your judgment. This chapter examines key aspects of how companies are valued. The next two chapters provide guidance for conducting your own analysis to help arrive at or confirm an existing valuation.

Getting a Head Start

Why try to make such investment-related determinations as part of the job-search process? After all, most job interviews don't turn into a real job because of some sort of a mismatch between the individual and the position being filled. Why not just wait until you receive an offer and evaluate the potential value of the stock options then?

The reason you need to start early is that by the time the offer comes, it will be too late to make any kind of informed judgment. You can't learn everything you need to know in a day or two or three. And that's typically the amount of time you have to make up your mind as to whether to accept a job offer.

So it's advisable to ask for relevant information all along the interview process, and to do additional research outside of the process. Asking the questions you need to ask can usually happen naturally as part of the meeting with your prospective employer. Invariably, you're encouraged by interviewers to inquire about the company that's interviewing you.

Now, it's important to get something clear right up front. I'm not urging you to begin a job interview by inquiring immediately about the value of stock options. If you do that, you'll likely turn off most employers. Such an approach is akin to asking a prospective employer questions about vacations and breaks before inquiring about what you'll be doing on the job.

As I noted in the previous chapter, you want to present yourself as an "option type employee." To do that, you need to demonstrate real expertise in your job area, and real passion for the kind of work you are looking to do.

The kinds of questions I suggest you focus on are described in more detail in the next chapter. As you'll discover, these questions have little to do with options, and more to do with the company's overall prospects and plans.

The nature of your questions may surprise company representatives, since your probing will likely be more incisive than that done by the typical job seeker. But rather than hurting your chances, such questioning will likely enhance the perception of you as a clear-thinking and informed individual. Indeed, if the kinds of questions you are asking put the company representatives off, then that is a danger signal in and of itself—that the company isn't as open as you'd like or doesn't have the answers to the questions you are asking. Both are bad signs in terms of answering the two questions posed at the start of this chapter.

The Game at Hand: Public vs. Private Companies

As a matter of background, it's important to appreciate that there's no single accepted way of valuing companies. Moreover, the process you go through can vary significantly from one company to another, depending on its history, ownership, and the amount of data available.

When it comes to valuing organizations, there are really two classes of companies.

Publicly-held companies

These are the easiest companies to value—in the *present*. You can go to any of dozens of Web sites or a daily newspaper and simply look up their value. It is stated on a per-share basis, say $12 per share. To come up with a total value for the company, you need to find out how many shares are outstanding (usually stated in the company's annual report, contained on many corporate Web sites), and then multiply the per-share price by the number of those outstanding shares. Thus, a company trading at $12 a share that has 10 million shares outstanding has a value (sometimes referred to as its "market capitalization") of $120 million.

The much more difficult task is valuing a publicly-traded company for the *future*. The reason this is so difficult is that its value can be subject to the conventional sorts of management issues—strategy, sales trends, promotional ability, etc. (discussed at length in Chapter 8)—plus such intangibles as what's "in" or "out" of favor on Wall Street.

There are individuals known as securities analysts, employed by investment banking, brokerage, and research firms, who spend days and weeks at a time assessing a company to come to conclusions about its likely future value. They interview members of the management team as well as industry experts and even customers and suppliers to gauge its business prospects.

You need to make some judgments about the future value of a company you're going to work for because any stock options you receive in a publicly-traded company are likely to be at the stock's price when you sign on. Thus, if you take a job with a company whose stock is trading at $12 a share, your options will likely be $12. The pricing is governed by the company's need to comply with tax laws, which require that the option price be based at a minimum on the company's actual value. Clearly, it's tougher to "fudge" a publicly-held company's value than a private company's value.

I experienced the difficulty associated with valuing a public company in the future when our Internet company was negotiating with prospective acquirers during 1999. One of the companies we had extensive discussions with was a small, publicly-held company that specializes in managing and extracting information from huge databases. Its stock had languished for about two years in the area of $2 to $4 a share. During the four months or so during which our on-again, off-again discussions proceeded, the stock was in the low part of the range, and actually dipped slightly under $2 a share a few times. Based on having 15 million shares outstanding, the company was being valued at about $30 million.

Its executives were interested in our company as an opportunity to reposition their firm as an Internet company. That seemed a reasonable goal, since the database company's existing technology was rapidly becoming obsolete thanks to the rapid movement of the Internet.

Our negotiations with that company broke down for two reasons: First, this other organization wanted to acquire us in exchange for stock options that, according to the existing value of the acquiring company, were perhaps one-fourth the value we saw in our company. Second, and perhaps most important, we weren't convinced that there were compelling reasons for the stock to go up.

At the time the negotiations broke down for good, there was one potentially encouraging development at the prospective acquirer: A new chief executive had been hired, who had previously led a fast-growing publicly-held company whose stock had risen sharply. However, he seemed disinclined so early in his tenure to aggressively pursue an acquisition.

So we explored other avenues. About three months after our discussions ended, I noticed that the stock of the data storage company began heading up, to $3, $4, $6, $8 . . . and finally to $17 a share. Its total value had risen by a factor of more than eight, from $30 million to $255 million. It turned out that there were rumors that the company might itself be acquired. When those rumors didn't pan out, the stock fell back to about $5 a share, still double the price when we were having our discussions.

But the lesson to me was that trying to predict the potential stock value of a publicly-held company is difficult at best, especially in today's volatile market, with day traders and online discussion groups exerting major influence. The force of rumors, for example, can provide powerful upward or downward pressure on stock prices. Technology companies, in particular, can swing wildly up and down, depending on the particular market forces at work at a particular point in time. And because options don't necessarily vest when you most want to sell shares, projecting the value of the shares of publicly-held companies at a particular point in time is dicey at best.

This isn't to say that trying to project a public company's future value is a useless exercise. By asking the questions posed in the next chapter, and obtaining informed answers, as discussed in Chapter 10, you can make reasonable judgments about the likely direction of a company's stock over the medium to long term.

Privately-held companies

When it comes to valuing private companies in the *present,* the owners are at an advantage. They can place any value they want on their companies and likely make a cogent argument in the their favor. If you'll recall in Chapter 4, when Johnny Sweetalker's lawyer questioned him about the value of Superfastgrowth.com, he asked Johnny that question under two separate scenarios—if he was trying to raise investment funds or if he was dealing with his wife's divorce lawyer. Of course, the valuations Johnny ascribed varied widely, and both his arguments sounded logical.

It's much more difficult for the founder of a publicly-held company whose shares are trading at $2 a share to argue that they really are worth $10 a share. You will likely ask, "Why doesn't the rest of the marketplace agree with you?"

I know one entrepreneur who lived the charade of a private company owner after helping found her software company in 1996. For a period of time, from early 1997 until the end of 1998, she valued her company, for "conversation purposes," at $3 million. When there was someone she especially wanted to hire, she would throw out that number, and point out that based on the 6 million shares outstanding, the value of her stock was 50 cents a share. Her stock options could be exercised mostly at a price of 10 cents a share (based on her official valuation of about $300,000). She always prefaced her viewpoint by emphasizing that the valuation was only her opinion, based on how other companies in her software sphere were being valued.

While this woman's software company came, by the start of the year 2000, to be worth considerably more than $3 million, it probably wasn't worth that much earlier on. However, only a few of the dozens of prospective employees she interviewed and offered stock options to ever probed enough to get her to justify such a valuation. Too bad.

If it turns out that owners are overvaluing the company, then they may be overvaluing the potential worth of the stock options. You, in turn, may be over-estimating the compensation value of options you receive. Going back to the previous example, if the likely value of the software company was closer to $2 million than $3 million, then any stock options had a real value more in the range of 33 cents a share than 50 cents a share—about one-third less. Options on 60,000 shares, then, would be worth about $20,000 rather than $30,000, representing a significant difference in compensation.

The Most Common Valuation Methods

Keep in mind that there is no single way to value a company. Even professionals like accountants and private investors have a hard time ascribing a value to a company. Here are some of the ways they do it:

■ *Valuing the assets, minus the liabilities.* This is the most straightforward way to value a company. Total up the value of the equipment, buildings, furniture, accounts receivable, and other assets, and subtract outstanding invoices, loans, accounts payable, and other liabilities.

One problem with this method is that it doesn't take into account the difficulty of valuing certain key assets, like customer lists, and proprietary items like software. Another probably more important problem is that this approach fails to take into account the realities of the marketplace. In other words, at what price are other companies of this sort being sold?

■ *Take a multiple of earnings.* This is how you used to hear publicly-held companies being valued. Thus, a company that has annual earnings (i.e. profits) of $1 a share and trades at $10 a share can be said to be trading at a multiple of 10 times earnings. Generally speaking, companies in specific established industries tend to trade at similar multiples; thus, companies in the paper manufacturing industry might trade at 10 times earnings, and companies in the airline industry might trade at 15 times earnings.

The earnings-multiple approach can then be applied to private companies. If you know that publicly-held companies in your industry are valued at a certain multiple, you can apply the same multiple to a private company. Thus, a privately-held paper manufacturer can be valued at the same earnings multiple that is applied to publicly-held companies, as a guidepost. (Of course, this assumes a private company is willing to disclose its profits.)

■ *Take a multiple of revenues.* The emergence of the Internet has made more popular an old approach to valuing companies—a multiple of revenues. Companies in the services sector in particular, such as direct mail or advertising agencies, have long been valued on the basis of annual revenues. Generally, they'll be acquired for the equivalent of one year's revenues or, if they are particularly desirable, perhaps 1.5 times one year's revenues.

Over the last few years, newly created Internet companies have been valued on the basis of revenues, sometimes at multiples of from three or four times revenues to even several hundred or a few thousand times revenues. The reasons for the wide variations have had to do with investors' judgments as to the long-term potential of the companies.

■ *Determine the price at which similar companies are selling.* Just as real estate agents look for "comparable sales" when trying to value a house for sale, so professionals in valuing a company examine the selling prices of "market equivalent" companies. The challenge with determining what other companies sell for is that the information often isn't available, unlike the prices of home sales, which are publicly posted by cities and towns as part of the public record of deeds and claims.

■ *Determine what private investors like venture capitalists paid for stock in the most recent round of investment.* For technology companies, in particular, this is an excellent way to get a fix on the company's current or recent valuation. If venture capitalists invested $10 million for one-fourth ownership of a company, then you can reasonably ascribe a value of $40 million to the company.

Professionals involved in valuing companies have other tools at their disposal, as well. They'll sometimes apply something called "discounted future cash flows" that seek to project the real value of likely future revenues and profits. They'll try to figure the value of a company operating as an independent entity, and as part of an acquiring company.

In the final analysis, of course, a company is only worth what someone else is willing to pay for it. In the real world of buying and selling companies, none of the approaches described previously is ever used exclusively. Rather, buyers and sellers debate the likely future accomplishments of the company in their efforts to negotiate a price. ■

Chapter 8

Ten Questions to Ask Before Accepting Equity Compensation

How do you know if a particular company will be a winner or a loser? Does it have what it takes to succeed? You can get a good idea by studying its business plan. What are the ten key questions to ask to help you decide whether to put your career and earning potential on the line? The answers will help you decide if the company is worth your investment.

Now that you understand the thinking behind valuing public and private companies in the *present*, it's time to probe more deeply into the factors that are most important in predicting value in the *future*.

If you've ever been involved in raising money from professional investors like venture capitalists, you know that when you first meet them, they ask lots of questions. They mostly inquire about the company's future—the sales projections, the market size, the strategy. They are trying, as they often put it, "to understand the business." In other words, does the business have what it takes to succeed in a big enough way to make the investors incredibly rich?

Since you as a prospective employee or contractor are an investor, you should ask similar questions as you move through the hiring process, especially if the company

89

in question is young, small, and not well known. You want to understand what it is that makes the business tick and what its chances are for success. Most important, you want to understand two things:

■ If this company represents an attractive medium-term (one to three years) investment.

■ The likely future value of the company's stock. In other words, what kind of appreciation can you expect in the price of the company's stock?

Why my focus on the one-to-three-year time horizon? Because that is the most realistic time period from both a career and investment viewpoint for you. We're not interested in get-rich-quick schemes here, nor are we interested in situations that extend beyond a time period for which it is reasonable to make informed projections.

A Shortcut to Obtaining Your Answers

Just because you ask the right questions doesn't mean you're going to get the answers you need. Most of the questions can't be answered easily or definitively. In some cases, the people you'll be asking won't have ready answers, or won't even have thought much about the questions. My intent in this chapter is to provide you with a list of key questions to ask, and to provide guidance in determining what you should be looking for in the way of answers.

One way to get a running start on answering your questions is to obtain a copy of a target company's overview slide presentation and/or its written business plan. Most privately-held fast-growth companies today have snappy PowerPoint slide presentations that they use to introduce themselves to prospective customers and investors—replete with company accomplishments, missions, and executive team descriptions. Many also have written plans because they are required by prospective investors and lenders, as well as by key strategic alliance partners.

90

Most publicly-held companies have written plans, as well, though they tend to include much more detail on operational matters like how the IT group will be organized or the kinds of incentives to be used by the sales department. Even if a publicly-held company doesn't have a formal plan, it will have documents about company performance and opportunities that it is required to file with the federal Securities and Exchange Commission; these documents (discussed in greater detail in the next chapter) are available on the Internet and in print for anyone to review.

Because written business plans usually contain proprietary information, such as about financial results, key customers, and marketing plans, companies don't just hand out their business plans to anyone who walks through the door. You'll need to determine, based on a number of both tangible and intangible factors, whether it's appropriate to ask for one.

One tangible factor governing your decision is how senior a position you are interviewing for. If you're potentially going to be part of the executive team, or reporting to a key member of the executive team, then it is definitely appropriate to request a copy of the business plan. But if you're going to be a junior member of the marketing or technical department, it may be less appropriate to ask for the business plan. If you do so, the employer may actually suspect you as a "plant"—someone sent by a competitor to spy on the employer.

An intangible factor governing your request for a business plan is simply how the "chemistry" of the interview process seems to be going. If it's clear during initial interviews that you're moving past formalities and into serious discussions, you may feel comfortable asking to review the business plan, in the context of fully understanding the company and its growth plans. You might add that you're willing to sign a confidentiality agreement, a short legal agreement most fast-growth companies have on hand, in which you promise not to disclose or steal the information you obtain.

In some cases, you'll be told that you and the company need to be closer to a decision about whether you'll be hired. In others, you'll be told that the plan "is being revised" and will be ready for you to review in a few weeks. And in still others, you'll be told that there isn't a plan, but that one is "in the works." You'll need to assess the tone and context of the answers you receive. If concern is expressed about making available financial projections or a lengthy plan, you can offer to review a copy of the plan minus the spreadsheets underlying the financial projections, or a summary version of the plan. Or possibly the company's basic slide presentation will do the trick for you. Your potential seriousness about the job as well as the company's seriousness about you should determine how hard you push on this matter.

Moreover, just because a company doesn't have a business plan doesn't mean you can't conduct your assessment. Nor does it mean that a company won't do well. Highly successful companies like Reebok International Inc. and Pizza Hut were started and grew for many years without business plans. One reality is that it's very difficult to write a business plan, and some companies sincerely mean to, but aren't able to complete one as quickly as they anticipate. If a business plan isn't available, you should take that as a potential warning sign, but be prepared to press on with your questions if you like what you've seen in the people you've met and the job situation for which you're being considered.

Even if you obtain a copy of a business plan, you'll still need to work hard to get your questions answered. The business plan will provide a running start, but it's not a crib sheet.

When I advise entrepreneurs about how to write a business plan, I always begin by telling them that a business plan is "a selling document." It is meant to sell prospective investors, strategic partners, suppliers, and key employees on the likely success of the business. (See my book about business planning, *How to Really Create a Successful Business Plan*, Inc. Publishing.)

As in any sales document, the information and assessments contained in a business plan are biased in favor of the company producing the document. Second, the document may not completely answer all of the questions you have, and may indeed raise more questions than it answers.

Stay Focused on the Real Issues

I have come up with ten key questions, not because there aren't more, but because I feel it's important in this kind of assessment to be focused on the most important issues. You are not trying to do what a professional valuation expert does. Nor are you trying to come up with some "magic number" of a company's value in three or four years. Rather, you are trying to make some reasonable assumptions within a reasonable amount of time about the potential value of stock options you will receive as part of a job offer.

Given such parameters, here are the questions I consider to be most important in assessing the potential value of a company:

1. *What is the management team's track record?*

The single most important ingredient in any company's ultimate success is the quality of its management team—the two to five people who make the key decisions about the company's direction. Seasoned venture capitalists will always tell you the following, or some variation: "Given the choice between a company with a first-rate management team with a second-rate product or one with a second-rate team and a really innovative product, I'll take the former."

The reason so much emphasis is placed on the management team is that it's people and their management abilities that ultimately determine whether a business will succeed. There are all kinds of examples of highly successful companies selling products that aren't necessarily the top ones available. The classic example is the dominance of the Microsoft Windows operating system in place of the Apple Macintosh system. Macintosh was for many years the superior product, but Microsoft's executives made more correct management decisions than Apple's.

How do you determine the likelihood of a management team's succeeding? You examine its track record. If the team worked together in another company, what did it accomplish in terms of sales growth? Where did it fall down?

If the team hasn't worked together before, then you should examine the accomplishments of its individual members. Where did they work most recently? What were their most important accomplishments? Ideally, you want to see examples of how the team or the individual members helped grow other companies, or groups within large companies. Remember, you are looking for winners.

If you find that the team or individual members exited from situations that didn't pan out, it doesn't mean they can't succeed, since failures sometimes are necessary before individuals can succeed. But failures or inconclusive results in the past are warning signs. For example, in all the hand-wringing and analysis about the implosion during 1999 of Value America, a former high-flying Internet department store, analysts pointed out that one of the founders, Craig Winn, had similarly led a lighting company during the seven previous years, and that it had eventually wound up in bankruptcy. People tend to repeat their patterns—in terms of both winning and losing.

Be especially wary if the company you are considering is reluctant to provide such information, or won't provide many details about the career paths of the key people.

2. *What is the company's strategy?*

A company's strategy is, quite simply, a statement of a company's overall approach to producing and selling its products and/or services, and how it plans to maximize its success. The term "strategy" suggests something highly conceptual, but the best strategies are specific and easy to understand. A promising strategy usually refers to how a company plans to take advantage of some new technology or product superiority or competitive advantage to exploit particular opportunities.

Be careful of companies espousing strategies that are full of buzzwords or puffery. High-tech companies, in particular, tend to express themselves in technical lingo.

Your challenge is to avoid falling into the trap of thinking that because you don't understand a company's strategy that the problem must be your lack of sophistication or business training. Don't be afraid to ask what seem to be silly questions—about the definition of a term or the meaning of a statement. (i.e. "We plan to leverage consumer trends to position ourselves to exploit recent paradigm shifts towards broadband information distribution.")

There's nothing wrong with saying that you don't understand what is being said, and that you would appreciate some clarification.

Professional investors judge companies partly based on how clearly and concisely the management team can explain the company's strategy. They sometimes refer to these quick explanations as "the elevator speech"—how well you can describe your company in the 30 seconds or so you have in a ride up an elevator with a VIP. If the people you're speaking with at a potential employer company can't explain its strategy in a way that you can understand, then you have a potential red flag. Because if they can't explain it easily to you, then they likely can't explain it easily to prospective investors and customers.

3. *What is the company's marketing plan?*

What you really want to know here is how well the company understands its market—the prospective customers. A marketing plan identifies precisely those groups it expects will become customers. These may be particular kinds of companies, such as those of a certain revenue range within a specific industry, or they may be particular consumers, like urban females age 20 to 40 or Baby Boomers with a particular health problem. How many of them are there? How quickly is the market growing? What are the difficulties associated with reaching the market? How does the company plan to overcome the difficulties?

A marketing plan also identifies how the company expects to reach its target customers. Will it advertise? Use public relations? Other types of promotion? How much will it spend on each of these activities? What does it expect in return? Equally important, especially if the company is a startup or launching a new product or service (especially one with which you are supposed to be involved): What evidence does it have that its offerings are what the market wants? Has it done any test marketing? What were the results? If not, has it conducted any surveys or focus groups? What were the outcomes? As much as possible, you want to see hard data that supports the claims of the marketing plan.

As much as possible, you want to answer this question: Does the market *really* need this product, or is it just another technology that someone thinks is "really cool"?

4. *Who are its competitors?*

Listen carefully to the answer to this question. If the answer is, "What we are doing is so unique that we don't have any competitors," be careful. Every company has competitors, even if they don't do exactly what your potential employer does. The competitors may be satisfying the market demand with a different type of product or service.

You want to hear the names of competitors, and a description of what they do.

At the same time, you want to hear a sense of respect for the competition. After all, savvy executives learn from the competition. If you hear the competition described in a contemptuous or dismissive way, take note. Your target company may be wearing dangerous blinders.

One other reason to inquire about the competition is to determine, if possible, how other similar companies are valued. If competitors include publicly-held companies, you can make such determinations.

5. *What is the company's competitive advantage?*

It's a given in today's hypercompetitive marketplace that any company that demonstrates even a bit of potential success will have competitors before long. Not all of them will succeed in a big way. The only ones that will succeed will be those that figure out a way to stand apart from the competition—based on better distribution, perceived product or service quality, lower prices or some other factor or combination of factors.

So you want to hear, hopefully without having to ask, what your target company feels it does better than the competition—its competitive advantage. In the best of all worlds, you'd learn that the company has a great patent that effectively shuts competitors out of the marketplace for the next 15-plus years. But because that's unlikely, you'll need, once again, to listen for logic and a sense of respect for the

97

competition. You want to hear specifically about how your company is putting systems in place and listening to its customers and planning to service customers over the long term more effectively than competitors. If the answer boils down to something like, "We're bigger than they are, so we'll blow them away," or "They're a bunch of bozos," watch out.

6. *How does the company sell its products and/or services?*

The single most important function in any company is sales. A company that can't figure out how to get customers to buy its products or services on a consistent basis won't go very far, no matter how creative or technically adept it might be.

You need to try to determine two things:

First, you want to know how the company's product or service is sold to actual users. Is it being sold via distributors, retailers, or directly by the company? How is the Internet being used? Increasingly, companies that act as intermediaries (like wholesalers or travel agencies) are being squeezed out by manufacturers or airlines that use the power of the Internet to reach end users directly.

Second, you want to have a sense of the skills of the people doing the selling. My feeling is that selling is a skill that is very difficult to learn and is more of a talent than anything else. Some people have sales personalities. They have a way of gaining people's trust and confidence. In other words, effective salespeople "are born, not made."

Once you get serious with a potential employer, you should consider requesting permission to sit through a typical sales presentation that the salespeople make to prospective customers. You'll see how they approach the process—whether they use product demonstrations or overhead slides—so you can make a determination of their professionalism. Ask yourself as you view a sales presentation: Would I be persuaded to buy from these people?

7. *How does the company promote itself?*

To help generate sales leads, a company has to find ways to get itself noticed in the marketplace. The most cost-effective way of doing this is via public relations—the process of calling attention to yourself through the media and other avenues like speaking engagements. Another more costly promotional tool is advertising.

What you want to know is this: How much attention is being given to promotion? What is the plan for using public relations, advertising, and other types of promotion? A company that expects to grow entirely by "word of mouth" or has the "Field of Dreams" philosophy ("Build it and they will come") probably isn't being realistic.

You can make some early determinations about promotion by reviewing a company's news releases on its Web site. How many are there? Who is the contact, an in-house person or a public relations agency? A company that is serious about promotion has usually engaged a public relations agency, unless it is a startup that can't yet afford an agency. But even in that situation, the company should be looking forward to the day when it can engage an agency.

Look also for signs of so-called "guerrilla marketing"—creative, low-cost ways to get the company's name out. Many small food companies, for example, have found ways to give samples out at key events (i.e. bottled water distributed at a road race). Some online companies have come up with creative contests that generate much attention. Not all promotion need be expensive and "by the rules."

8. *What is the company's financial condition?*

Here's an area where you may feel out of your league. Don't. You need not be an accountant to be able to evaluate whether a company is in decent financial condition or not.

99

Most important, you want to determine that the company isn't really on the verge of running out of money and going out of business. But beyond that, you want to know that the company has enough cash on hand that it really can implement all the plans you likely learned about by asking the previous questions. Here are some questions you can ask to get at the issue:

What is the company's historical sales trend? Ideally, you want to see revenues heading up sharply over the most recent two or three years.

Has the company raised any investment funds or borrowed money? You should be able to gain some sense of the amount of money raised, and how much has been spent.

How much cash does the company have on hand? The best way to phrase this question is something like, "Into how many weeks or months worth of operations does the company's cash position translate?" In other words, how long could the company continue operations if sales suddenly slowed? Venture capitalists refer to this as the company's "burn rate."

Ideally, you'd like to get a peek at the company's three main financial statements—its income statement (sometimes referred to as the "profit-loss statement"), balance sheet, and cash flow statement—for the most recent two or three years, and projected ahead two or three years. These are usually contained in a company's business plan. Here you can see what the revenue trend has been, whether the company is making or losing money, and what its expectations are for the future. From the balance sheet, you can determine the company's cash situation, along with how much it is owed by customers, and how much it owes to vendors.

If you get hold of the company's financial statements and feel totally incompetent to review them, consult with a friend or relative who may have some financial experience, or with your accountant. Once again, you're not looking to do a detailed financial analysis, but rather to determine overall trends.

9. How well does the product or service "scale"?

This is a question that prospective investors like to ask because it really gets at the question of how quickly the company can grow. You are trying to determine whether there are ways to satisfy market demand aside from simply adding people. For a manufacturing company, an obvious way to "scale" is to make the equipment operate faster, or add more equipment, so more widgets can be produced more quickly.

One of the reasons many Internet stocks have done so well is because of the visions of scalability that investors have. For a retailing Web site, for example, there's no need to add more sales clerks and rent more store space if business increases substantially. All that may be necessary is a larger computer server. At the Internet company I helped found, one of our key methods for achieving scalability is to use e-mail; the more e-mails a company wants distributed, the more it pays. However, there's no substantial difference in labor or materials costs associated with sending 50,000 e-mails or 300,000 e-mails.

So inquire into how the company expects to achieve scalability. It will need to demonstrate an ability to scale if it is going to grow as quickly as necessary to drive its value price up sharply.

10. What is the "exit strategy"?

You want to know how you're going to realize the value of your stock options—when you can "cash out," as it is sometimes expressed. As long as a company remains privately held, in the hands of one or a few owners, employees holding stock options have no viable way to sell any stock they may purchase so as to realize gains that may have resulted from an increase in a company's value. The stock is said to be "illiquid."

You want your company's owners to have a clear vision of how they and prospective shareholders like yourself are going to be put into a position to sell stock in the company—to be made "liquid." As discussed in Chapter 6 about "Equity Sweet Spots," there are two main ways to provide liquidity: The company goes public or the company is acquired.

One other question you want to ask as a part of your inquiry into the exit strategy: What is the timing? Ideally, the timing should be within the next one to three years.

If the timing sounds vague—"as we get closer to retirement," or "if someone comes along and makes us an offer we can't refuse"—be careful. You may be dealing with entrepreneurs—and there are many of them—who are more interested in retaining control than in cashing out. Unbelievable as it may seem, lots of entrepreneurs are much more interested in running their own show over a long period of time than in maximizing the value of their stock over the intermediate term. If their goals conflict with yours, try to find out sooner rather than later, since they ultimately decide whether a company goes public or is sold.

The answers to these questions won't necessarily give you a precise future valuation for a company, but they will provide you with the information and insights to help determine whether stock in the company represents a viable investment. One way to further hone in on the possible future value of the company is to examine how other companies in the same industry are being valued. If you're considering a company that develops e-commerce software, you can see how other e-commerce companies have been valued in the marketplace. Examine how some of the more established ones have performed over a one-to-three-year time frame.

The more convincing the answers, the likelier it is that the value of the company will rise substantially over the next one to three years. ∎

Chapter 9

Negotiating Strategies: How Many Options Should You Receive?

*Negotiating for options is a new but essential art. Even
though you're dealing with a lot of "what ifs," you still need to
try to place a reasonable value on the options. You also
need to determine how much leverage you have. If you're
being recruited and have other offers, you have more
leverage than if you're pushing to get in the door. Learn a
step-by-step negotiating strategy for staying focused on the
issues that matter most.*

L ove is a'bloomin'. You've decided that you
want to work for a particular company,
and it's making noises like it wants to
make you a job offer. You've been told
that options are, well … an option. What's
the next step on the path to settling on the
deal?

The size of any options package is a matter of
negotiation, just like the size of your salary and other
benefits. Too often, people treat options as an afterthought—
"a piece of paper."

That was the attitude Paula Jagman had back in 1994,
when she joined Internet company UUNET as an executive
assistant and received $32,000 in annual salary and stock

options for 25 cents a share. "To me, the stock market was reserved for people who had lifetime subscriptions to *The Wall Street Journal,*" she says. "You know, it was a language. It was something that, you know, low-income families didn't even begin to understand."

Of course, her attitude changed in 1995, when the stock went public at $26 a share and her stock options were suddenly worth $3 million. "The very first thing we did was we paid off my mom's mortgage, and I spent $25,000 fixing up her house." Had Paula been better informed, she might have been able to negotiate a larger number of options, and made even more money.

I encountered employees at the Internet company I helped found who had the same difficulties as Paula comprehending the significance of options. I recall one programmer who, when we were negotiating his salary, explicitly pushed for more money over a larger options package. "I can't pay the rent with the options," he said. As he discovered when the company was sold, he could buy a lot more than rent with the proceeds from the options.

Once you appreciate the potential financial power of options, you're ready to examine where they fit into your compensation. How do you go about negotiating your options package? You need to find ways to attach a value to two things:

1. The gain on the stock you could obtain via the options;

2. To yourself as someone who could be instrumental in increasing the value of the stock.

Attaching a Value to the Options

Ideally, you'd like to be able to value the options as you do your compensation—for example, "These options look to be equal to about $25,000 of compensation this year, $40,000 next year, and $50,000 in year three."

Attaching an annual compensation figure to the options is not a simple matter, for several reasons:

■ Company valuation is a moving target; it can increase or decrease depending on a company's month-to-month fortunes.

■ You don't get the stock right away—remember from Chapter 4, the options typically "vest" over three to five years.

■ There's a much greater element of risk than with your salary. Sure, the options could be worth a small (or large) fortune in the future, but they could also be worth nothing in a year or two.

Thus, you're dealing with both inherent complexity and a great many "what ifs" (what if I leave before the options vest, what if you've overstated the current value of the company, what if the company goes public and the value of the shares increases by 100 times, and so on and so forth). Largely because of the complexity and the "what-ifs," I believe strongly that there's much to be said for a simple approach: attaching a compensation value to the options based on their likely current value, and reasonable expectations of appreciation in value going forward. Otherwise, you are susceptible to all kinds of "blue sky" arguments—"Gee, if we go public, your 50,000 shares could be worth $50 a share and you'd be worth $2.5 million. How's that for compensation?" Everyone knows that the reason you as an employee or contractor accept options is because you have a reasonable expectation that the options will have significant value in the future, and perhaps very significant value.

In a Private Company

Thus, as noted in the previous chapter, if you feel that a company has a current value of 50 cents a share, and the stock options would cost you 10 cents a share, you could reasonably value your compensation via options at 40 cents a share. If you feel the shares will likely be worth $1.00 a share after one year, you could reasonably value your options compensation at another 50 cents a share the second year.

In this scenario, 60,000 stock options could be valued at $24,000 the first year ($30,000 minus the $6,000 cost of the stock) and $30,000 the second year (the additional 50 cents per share of appreciation in the value of the stock). Obviously, the stock could be worth much more. But remember, you as an employee wouldn't have access to any of the stock during your first year, in any event. If the stock vests over three years, you would only be eligible to purchase 20,000 shares after the first year, 20,000 shares after the second year, and 20,000 shares after the third year, until you had the entire 60,000 shares.

In a Public Company

What if you are dealing with options in a company that is already publicly held? Let's say you are being offered options to buy for $10 a share stock that is trading on a stock exchange at $10 a share. In that situation, it makes sense to examine the stock's past performance. How much has it increased (or decreased) in value over the last six months, one year, two years, and so forth?

If the stock has been increasing in value 50% a year for each of the last three years, then it may be fair to apply that increase to future years. After year one, it's reasonable to assume the stock would be worth $15, after year two $22.50, and after year three $33.75. That gives you a potential gain of $5 a share after year one, another $7.50 a share after year two, and $11.25 in year three. Multiply each of those numbers by the number of shares, and you have a way of measuring the potential compensation value of the options.

Just remember, this approach isn't foolproof in any way. It is merely one guide. Another approach could include measuring only the gain on each year's vested stock at the time it becomes available. In this approach, options that vest over three years wouldn't be considered to have any value when you join a company, and would only have a value at the end of each year, when you could actually acquire a certain number of shares.

Attaching a Value to Yourself

You may be more valuable than you think. In today's job market, with the unemployment rate having dipped under 2% in some areas of the country, the biggest problem facing many young growing companies—companies with equity that is likely to increase sharply in value—is finding the people they need. As I pointed out in Chapter 1, entrepreneurs have become increasingly generous in making equity available to employees, not because the companies have suddenly become more charitable, but because they are reacting to a marketplace in which labor is a scarce resource.

So the key question you need to ask yourself as you become serious with a potential employer is this: *How vital are you to this company?*

The more vital you are, the more valuable a package you can negotiate.

Of course, from the viewpoint of you, the prospective employee, the hardest part of the process is determining just how valuable you are, and how determinedly you can hold out. Keep in mind, however, that negotiating options isn't necessarily a onetime affair. If you determine that your value to the company you have joined is higher than you originally thought, you can, as part of your salary review process, attempt to negotiate additional options. You generally have less leverage at this point, since you are already employed and it would likely be a hassle to leave, but especially valuable employees have used this approach to add to their options package.

109

Here are the two likeliest scenarios that will help you determine your value:

1. *You're being recruited.* This is the preferred scenario, since it tends to increase your value. Perhaps the company has heard about you, and has targeted you as perfect for a particular spot. Or it has hired a recruiting firm (headhunter) to fill a spot, and the recruiting firm has recommended you. In the latter situation, you may have offers from other companies via the recruiting firm, as well.

If such a situation comes to pass, you're in the catbird seat. You are being coveted, and you can play hard-to-get. In any negotiation, the easier it is for you to say no, the more leverage you have.

For a graphic illustration, look at George Shaheen, who in 1999 left the chief executive position at Andersen Consulting, which paid him an estimated $4 million in annual salary and bonus, to take a job with an Internet-based grocery distributor, Webvan. According to the Feb. 7, 2000, issue of *Fortune,* he received an annual salary of "only" $750,000, but he was able to negotiate for 5% of Webvan in stock and options. By early 2000, about six months after Shaheen joined Webvan, the company had gone public, and his stock-option package was worth in excess of $90 million.

2. *You're in search of a job.* Increasing numbers of people want to work for "dot-coms" and other potentially fast-growing companies. They apply to Yahoo!, Amazon.com, Lycos, and other "name" Internet companies, not to mention other technology companies like Microsoft and Hewlett-Packard in droves. These companies have a seemingly insatiable appetite for people. But, not surprisingly, these companies have many more applicants than they could ever hire, so they can afford to be highly selective.

What that means is that if you are fortunate enough to be offered a job, it will more likely be with the salary and

110

options package pretty well fixed. Sure, if you've managed to entice the company with your skill set and you fill an important hole, and/or you have another job offer, you may be able to increase the salary and options offer some. But you won't have nearly the same kind of leverage as someone in the first category, who's being actively pursued.

The Going Rates for Senior Executives

If you're a candidate for a senior executive position at a fast-growing company and you're being actively recruited, there are some guidelines that recruiting firms and investors use for how much the individuals should expect to receive in stock options:

■ *President and CEO:* 6%-10% of the company's stock. The actual percentage usually depends on the company's stage and stability when the new CEO signs up. The earlier in the company's formation the new CEO signs on, the higher the percentage is likely to be. Executives with "cache"—well-known track records of success who can help convince venture capitalists to invest—have maximum leverage.

■ *Senior vice presidents:* 1%-3% of the company's stock. Generally speaking, those with a marketing and sales pedigree are rewarded toward the higher range and those with a financial orientation toward the lower range. That's because top-notch marketing and sales executives are just harder to find, and when they succeed, they add significantly to the revenue line. Financial executives are essential to reassure investors, but they can't usually make a claim to increase sales.

■ *Vice presidents and key managers:* .5%-2% of the company's stock. A vice president of sales or a manager of technology would be likelier to command the higher end of this range, while a vice president of finance or manufacturing would probably be at the lower end. As

111

described with senior vice presidents, those with marketing and sales expertise have the greatest amount of leverage. Executives and managers below these senior levels usually receive something less than .5%.

It is important to point out that these percentages can be misleading, and I advise job seekers to use the guidelines with care. The actual percentage of a company you receive in options is much less important than its potential value. Having 10% of a company that's unlikely to exceed $1 million in value is much less desirable than having 1% of a company that has a good chance of being worth $100 million.

Negotiating the Best Deal

For most people, negotiating is an unpleasant chore. It generally involves a certain degree of conflict, disagreement, and uncertainty—things most of us would just as soon avoid. Some people avoid negotiating by taking either of two actions: accepting what the other party is offering, or rejecting it completely and quickly moving on to other options. Either action does you a disservice. Most significant transactions—and a job is certainly a significant transaction—are negotiable.

Because negotiating is such a difficult chore for many people to handle, all kinds of advice exists, spelling out special approaches. Indeed, entire books and courses about negotiating tactics and strategies have been created.

I don't want to develop a treatise for negotiating. For purposes of negotiating a job offer involving options, my approach to negotiating can be embodied in two brief viewpoints:

1. You gain negotiating leverage to the extent you are willing to walk away from a potential deal.

2. Any agreement should be beneficial and comfortable to both parties, since it is the start of a long-term relationship. In other words, to the extent one party feels "ripped off," the negotiated arrangement will run into trouble down the line.

These two points may seem contradictory at first glance. If you have lots of leverage and negotiate a tough deal, then you run the risk of alienating the other party. As a new employee, the effect may be to create unrealistic expectations, as in: "If we're paying her $150,000 a year and giving her 100,000 stock options, she'd better walk on water." In reality, both sides to a negotiation must in the final analysis rely on their own personal judgment of what feels right. If you use all your leverage and are able to negotiate a truly extraordinary deal, but feel that you'll be asked to "walk on water," it may be best to take something a little less than extraordinary, or else to seek out different pastures.

Given the inherent difficulties associated with negotiation, and the complexities of negotiating employment arrangements layered with stock options, I want to emphasize that there isn't a single approach to negotiating. Here are several suggestions for helping the process along.

■ *Know your value.* Go into a job negotiation with a clear idea of what you are worth on the open market. In other words, what kind of salary could you reasonably expect to earn based on your skills and experience? This should be a number that doesn't have anything to do with stock options— it's just a cash figure. For example, if you are a Web developer with three years' experience with a well-known Web design firm, you may legitimately command a salary as high as $80,000.

■ *Finalize your salary first.* When negotiating a job offer, try to negotiate salary arrangements before discussing options. The idea here is to take the approach that's recommended for buying a new car. First, get the final price of the car, equipped as you'd like. Then, negotiate the trade-in of your old car. If you try to negotiate both together, you may find yourself with a fuzzy bottom line. That's because you're dealing with two different types of items. A new car has a "sticker" price (that few people pay) and a final real-world price that dealers try to manipulate. If you want to know the true value being offered for the trade-in, you should first know the real-world new-car price, since that is the easier item to value. Valuing an older car as a trade-in is much more difficult because each car comes in a different state of usage and repair.

Here's how the approach works in job negotiations. If you figure you're worth $150,000 in salary, and a highly promising company offers you $75,000 in salary, then you should be trying to obtain another $75,000 in compensation via stock options (based on the current value of the stock). As I've discussed, arriving at a determination of $75,000 for the value of options is a matter of some judgment and debate—not unlike trying to value a used car. If you were to get the options package first, with all kinds of razzle-dazzle about its current and likely future value, you'd be susceptible to taking a lower salary than you might otherwise deserve. You want to value the item that can be most easily valued— in your case, the job's salary—and leave the more difficult item until later.

Some employers will offer a complete package— salary, options, and other benefits—at the time they make you an offer. There is nothing wrong with this. Just be sure in your own assessment that you separate the salary from stock options.

■ *Do your due diligence.* In other words, try to be as informed as possible about how badly you are needed, as well as about the state of the company. The company may tell you you're one of four candidates, which can be scary. But if you know the position has been vacant for three months, you know that it's been a tough position to fill. If you know that three people have held the position over the

114

last six months, you also know that there may be a work-related problem, such as a difficult boss. More about due diligence follows in the next chapter.

■ ***Determine what others are receiving.*** One thing you definitely want to avoid is being shortchanged compared to what others in the company are receiving for options packages. Companies usually develop an overall approach or style to handing out stock options. That is, they make a certain amount of options available to new employees according to such factors as position and salary. The more established the company is, the more systematized the approach is likely to be. For example, increasing numbers of companies maintain "option budgets" that lay out the expected number of options set aside for various job categories.

The easiest way to find out about option budgets or overall approaches is to ask. This isn't something you ask in the first interview, but if you are getting more seriously engaged in the selection process with a particular company, you can certainly inquire about the company's approach to options. If the answer is, "Yes, we have an options program," you might ask for some insights into how options are valued and parceled out, so as to get the discussion going. If the person managing your interview process doesn't know, ask who would be the best person from whom to learn more. More established companies may have a director of human resources, who can explain the approach and rationale for handing out options. Also, if the company is publicly held, you can probably determine how many options the top four or five executives have by reviewing annual meeting and public offering statements that must be filed with the federal Securities and Exchange Commission. There are a variety of Internet resources you can use to search out such information, which you'll find in the next chapter.

If you're dealing with an early-stage company, the policies may not be very clear. In this situation, the options approach is probably still being worked out. This is actually an opportunity if you know what you're doing—especially if you can provide your own input as to what other companies in the same industry are doing on the options front. Based on the advice of the previous chapters, you should be inquiring into the company's possible valuation and making some judgment about what you might seek for options.

■ *Be prepared to negotiate hard on the options.* There's nothing that says you must accept the first offer. That may be the final offer, but you should be told that, rather than assuming it. Certainly it helps to have some ammunition behind your request for more options than you are being offered. If the company says it's offering you 30,000 options, to simply request 50,000 without any reason won't go very far. It helps much more to be able to say something like, "The options you are offering, from what I can determine, are worth about $15,000 in salary this year. You are offering me $60,000, so the compensation package is worth $75,000. But I know I could command $90,000 in this marketplace. That means I should be receiving twice as many options."

You may not get exactly what you are seeking, but you may be able to increase the offer. Remember, for most companies, it's easier to hand out more options than money. I know of one professional who was being actively recruited by a major Internet portal, and settled on a salary that was about 25% lower than what he knew he was worth. But he knew the range of options being offered to someone in his category, and he pushed hard for the maximum number of options possible. A year later, when those options began vesting, the stock appreciation made his first year's options worth double his salary. In the final analysis, you need to decide how badly you want the job and to work for the company in question as part of your decision.

116

■ ***Try to keep negotiations focused on the present rather than the future.*** When discussing stock options, the tendency by employers will be to get you to think about the potential value of the options, rather than the current value. The idea is to get you dreaming a little. ("Gee, just imagine if the company goes public and those 30,000 options are suddenly worth $20 a share.") Your goal should be to keep the discussion in the present tense. ("Yes, that's all well and good about $20 a share, but what I'm trying to do is determine what the stock is really worth today.")

■ ***Gain a commitment to renegotiate.*** Any options package you accept isn't necessarily frozen in concrete. It can be changed over time. Some companies will tell you that right from the start. If this isn't stated, try to obtain a commitment from the company to negotiate additional stock options at the time you come up for salary review (assuming they're warranted as part of additional compensation). You won't have the same leverage once you are onboard, but depending on how much you are valued, you will be able to negotiate additional options over time. Indeed, if you like the outlook for your employer, you may want to try to negotiate more options and less money as the basis of a compensation increase.

■ ***Remember, everything is negotiable.*** Companies would like you to think that much of their options package, like the vesting periods, is standard. The reality is that most aspects of stock options deals are negotiable. For example, it's possible for options to vest in accordance with meeting performance goals, like completing a high-priority project on schedule, instead of or in addition to time-based vesting.

Just because equity compensation is more complex and more difficult to understand than money doesn't mean you shouldn't try to get yourself the best possible deal. Equity compensation really is a form of money. It is valued

as such every day on stock markets around the world.
Nobody will work as hard on your behalf as you! ■

Chapter 10

Get the Information You Need for Wise Decision Making

To fully answer all your questions about an employer's business prospects, you're going to have to do some digging. If the company is privately held, you'll do one kind of digging, and if it's publicly held, you'll do another kind of digging. In either case, you'll want to know the inside poop on the top executives, and what employees, vendors, and customers really think about the company. Here are the resources and investigative techniques to make sure your digging is productive.

I've discussed assessing and valuing prospective companies. I've also pointed out how difficult it is to develop a complete portrait, assuming you have all the information you need.

However, you can be sure you won't have all the information you need based solely on what a prospective employer tells you, even if it makes available its slide show, business plan, annual report, and various marketing documents. There is additional relevant information you should learn, both positive and negative, about every company, no matter how well managed it might seem to be. For example, you'd like to know how other employees feel about working there so that you have a good sense of the working environment and related level of

119

politics. You'd like to know how it treats its vendors and suppliers, as an indication of how it treats people in general. You'd like to know if the company has been in legal trouble—who initiated the event and the nature of the charges—and how the situation was resolved (a settlement, a judgment, a fine, etc.)

How do you obtain the information you need to make an informed judgment? You need to do research. Fortunately, in this age of the Internet, there is much more information readily available than ever before. You can search through government documents, news clippings, investment analyst reports, and other important items right online.

In this chapter, I provide guidance for obtaining the information you need, from three perspectives:

1.   General approaches to carrying out research.
2.   Special approaches for researching privately-held companies.
3.   Special approaches for researching publicly-held companies.

General Research Approaches

What are you trying to accomplish? Most fundamentally, you want, as much as possible, to fill in the blanks of the questions I posed in Chapter 8—about the company's business prospects.

You want to obtain a "picture" of the company. You want to know about key trends concerning sales, hiring, finances, and so forth. You want to know what key decisions the company has made of late, and what key decisions it faces.

My feeling, based on many years in business, is that people tend to repeat themselves. Those who treat people shabbily or dishonestly usually do so repeatedly. Those who make poor judgments about markets or who are bad with numbers tend not to outgrow those habits. To put it perhaps a bit crudely: Losers tend to stay losers, and winners tend to repeat their winning ways.

The clearer the picture you draw, the better your decision is likely to be. Is this company right for you? Is it heading in the right direction? Most important in terms of any equity stake you may obtain, does it make for a good investment?

To obtain the required information to gain a clear picture, you need to take on the role of investigator. It's a role I'm familiar with from my years as a newspaper reporter with *The Wall Street Journal*. A newspaper reporter is basically an investigator. In addition to obtaining the "insider's" view of what's occurring in a company, a financial reporter wants to know what "outsiders" say.

An investigator uses two primary resources: *secondary* and *primary* sources. Secondary sources are mostly publications like newspapers, books, and magazines. Primary sources are individuals with whom you speak directly.

Accessing secondary resources has been made much easier than it once was with the advent of the Internet. The Internet is not only easily accessible—saving trips to libraries and government offices—but it holds vast troves of data. One example is the Internet-based "collection" of back issues of major newspapers and magazines. Until just a few years ago, only reporters and editors had access to in-house newspaper libraries containing clippings from dailies like *The Washington Post* or *The Boston Globe*, searchable by company and individual name. Now, anyone can log on and for either a nominal fee (usually $2 or $2.50 per full article), or in some cases for no charge at all, search through many years of previous issues.

In addition to searching out the Internet, you should be prepared to seek out and speak with appropriate individuals a company may be less than inclined to introduce you to. These may include present and former customers, vendors, directors, and employees.

Searching Private Companies

The startup and early-stage companies that offer the greatest likelihood of big equity payoffs are also most likely to be privately held. In other words, they are owned by one or a few people, unlike publicly-held companies, which are owned by hundreds or even thousands of individuals and whose shares are traded on stock exchanges. As the term implies, privately-held companies tend to be private about the information they make available to the general public. They often won't disclose such basic financial information as sales, number of employees, or if they're profitable.

The dearth of readily available information about private companies makes them more of a research challenge for a potential job seeker. From investigative and investment perspectives, though, I like to think about private companies as more potentially lucrative. If you do your homework, you may find important information that others have overlooked or have not been made aware of—information that can help you spot a potentially attractive investment opportunity via stock options or other equity incentives.

Here are key resources for investigating private companies:

■ *A company's Web site.* It's truly amazing what you can sometimes discover from a company's own Web site. Many now include information that was once considered highly proprietary—names of key customers and listings of all job openings. Companies are making such information available in significant measure as a response to ever-more-competitive sales and employment markets; they want to impress prospective customers about their existing customers and prospective employees about the wonderful opportunities available. One approach I find useful when investigating a company is to review its press releases distributed to the media. Many companies now post these announcements of new products, customers, and financing and banking arrangements, so reviewing them over a period of six months or a year can provide an excellent chronology of key company events.

■ *Internet search engines.* Punching a company name into several of the major search engines (i.e. AltaVista.com, GoTo.com, Dogpile.com) is a little more of a "needle-in-a-haystack" approach, but it is worth doing. The challenge is that such searches can yield hundreds or even thousands of listings. Foraging through all of them can be a tedious matter, since the one or two that are of greatest interest to you may be at the very end. However, this is usually a necessary first step toward determining what outsiders are saying about the company in question. Using this method, you're likely to come across media reviews of the company's products and services, information on the organization's retail and/or wholesale outlets, and comments about the company by financial experts, among other listings. The actual mix will depend on exactly what your target company does for a living.

■ *Newspapers and magazines.* The ability to search back issues of a growing number of newspapers and magazines represents a huge advance for anyone doing research on private companies because such efforts can yield a bonanza of information. Since you are searching for a specific company name, the searching process tends to be productive in the sense that you know early on whether or not there are results. The beautiful thing about searching newspapers and magazines is that a single article can provide not only an outside perspective, but often the names of outsiders who are familiar with your company, such as employees, suppliers, and members of the board of directors, since reporters like to quote the largest possible variety of individuals in their own research. The main challenge is to hone in on the most appropriate publications to search. Generally speaking, you should be searching according to geographic location and industry. Thus, if you are seeking information about an early-stage biotechnology company in Cambridge, MA, you'd be well advised to search back issues of *The Boston Globe*, as well as magazines and newsletters that report on biotechnology companies. The main limitation you are likely to encounter is that the smaller the publication, the less likely it is to have its database available via the Internet. In some cases, however, the publication will conduct a special search and inform you as to which back issue contained information about your target company—and then sell you that issue for a premium price—perhaps 25% to 50% more than its normal per-issue price. Vertical trade publications make it a practice to cover the cutting-edge technology of the industries they cover. Searching through them online can be valuable for learning whether your prospective employer has the competitive advantage it may be claiming to have.

■ *Court records.* One of the great "finds" from your search of newspapers, magazines, and newsletters can be a reference to a court case of some kind. Once you know about a court case, you can in most cases gain access to key documents that are part of that case—transcripts of testimony, motions for injunctions, defense responses, and so forth—since they are considered "public record." The nature of cases will tell you a lot up front—a spate of sexual harassment charges or vendor grievances against your company suggest a company with some problems in how it treats employees or outsiders. Moreover, whether they are plaintiffs or defendants, companies will often reveal quite sensitive information in the course of court cases about employment policies and business strategies. Newspaper reporters discover some of the most revealing material about companies in court records, and you should, too.

■ *Online database services.* A number of information databases maintain financial and other data on as many businesses as they can, including large numbers of private companies. Best known among these is Dun & Bradstreet (www.dnb.com). It claims to have information about more than 57 million businesses in 200 countries. Here, for less than $100, you can access the history and business background, and supplier-related information, of individual companies. The main drawback I've found with D&B and other such services is that the information can be incomplete or inaccurate. I know that as a business owner, I have avoided providing information I considered to be proprietary (such as my company's sales or number of employees) to D&B. Some business owners actually provide inaccurate information—usually exaggerating sales or numbers of employees in an effort to boost their images and credibility. In sum, consider accessing such information if you are very serious about working for a particular company, but accept the data with a grain of salt, comparing what you learn to what you are gleaning from other sources.

■ *Patents and trademarks.* The U.S. Office of Patents and Trademarks contains records of applications and awards of patents and trademarks. Here you can check out the truth of what you may have been told by company officials about important patents and trademarks. You can even scan the application forms to see how your company answered key questions, especially concerning the technical aspects of prospective patents. If you're a technical type, you may be able to make some judgments about the uniqueness of and creativity underlying patents.

■ *Present and former employees.* In any company research, especially on a smaller company, it helps to be able to talk to sources not recommended by the individuals who have been interviewing you. These people need not be in the area of the company where you'll be working, though it helps if they have some familiarity with it. You'll often gain a different perspective of the company from what your interviewers are hoping to project. How do you locate such people? Usually via friends, or friends of friends. I've been telephoned by potential employees of companies that I've been involved with as an employee or consultant, and have tried to help the individuals gain a clearer picture of the company and its prospects. In these calls, you should be trying to confirm information you've been given—perhaps about why a key employee is leaving or what a reorganization means or how sales of a particular product have been going. And, of course, you want a sense of how the company treats its employees, and how it rewards success, such as via stock options. Without a connection or reference, it is hard to make such calls anonymously, since employees likely won't trust you enough to talk frankly and openly. One other approach is to ask the target company if you might speak to one or more outside members of its board of directors or board of advisors. These people are obviously biased in favor of the company, but they are more distant and objective because they aren't there every day, and are supposed to act more as advisors than as executives. They will often be helpful in providing a sense of how well the company is doing and how realistic the company's objectives really are. At our online agency, we encouraged a number of prospective employees to speak with individual members of our board of advisors. Sometimes the employees came back at us with additional questions related to information we might not have made available—about future sales projections, for example—simply because the advisors were being candid.

■ *Customers and suppliers.* Individuals at customer and supplier companies have a unique perspective on the companies they deal with in either role. Companies that aren't responsive to customers or treat their suppliers with disdain likely have internal problems that could hurt their growth prospects. Once again, individuals tend to repeat behavior patterns. An executive who has been a micromanager in one situation is likely to be the same in the next situation. Your challenge in this arena may be locating customers or suppliers. Customers are usually quite willing to discuss their opinions of companies serving them, since the customers have little to lose. Suppliers, however, are likely to be more guarded, since they don't want unfavorable statements to somehow get back to their customer, and possibly endanger the relationship. Once again, your network of personal contacts—friends and friends of friends—is your best bet for locating candidates to speak with.

Key question: Has the private company received financing? As you'll recall, in Chapter 6, about equity sweet spots, I advised searching out companies that have recently received private investments, such as from venture capital firms. In your research, try to answer this question for yourself. Publications like *Red Herring* are especially helpful for providing leads in this area.

Searching Public Companies

Public companies are just that—highly public. Under government laws and rules, publicly-held companies are required, from the moment they decide to go public, to promptly disclose all information that is "material"—that is, information that could affect how they are viewed by investors. This information includes everything from quarterly revenues and earnings to senior executive appointments to significant new contracts. As a result, there is usually a treasure trove of information about public companies, especially in comparison to private companies.

The ready availability of information about public companies is both good news and bad news. It's good news because it means you can readily access lots of data about a particular company. You can learn about its history, financial performance, and the backgrounds of the key executives. You can also determine what investment experts are saying about the company and often locate lots of media commentary.

It's bad news because everyone else has access to the same information. That makes it much more difficult for you to be among just a few people to gain access to important information that could spell huge gains in a company's value. Any options you receive in a publicly-held company will be at the then-current market price—a price based on how those in the financial community value a company, as opposed to options in a private company, which are usually based on a more arbitrary price.

This isn't to suggest that it isn't possible to score big with options for shares in a publicly-held company. If you obtain enough options in a company whose shares increase significantly, you can do quite well. As you do your research, you need to assume more the role of stock picker than of investor.

In researching publicly-held companies, you should note that all of the resources listed under the previous section on private companies are applicable. In addition, here are four key resources you should access to learn more about particular publicly-held firms:

■ *The Securities and Exchange Commission (SEC).* The SEC is the federal agency charged with protecting investors via administration and enforcement of the nation's securities laws. Among the requirements of the securities laws are that companies regularly and fully disclose key data and developments about their operations, most notably financial results. The SEC acts as the repository of this information, which is cloaked in government regulation jargon—10-K (annual report), 8-K (change in material status), and so forth. This information is available via the SEC's Web site (www.sec.gov), and its EDGAR (Electronic Data Gathering, Analysis, and Retrieval system) database.

■ *Investment services and brokerage firms.* Publicly-held companies are often carefully researched by professional investment analysts of all types, such as those from investment services and brokerage firms. These analysts conduct the kind of research I advocate you conduct on private companies, and then some. They interview members of the management team, assess products, and talk to key stakeholders like suppliers and customers. Their written analyses can save you lots of work. Some of these analyses are readily available via the Internet (sometimes for free and sometimes for a charge), but some are only made available to customers of full-service brokerage firms.

■ *Internet message boards.* These are Internet sites that offer investors the opportunity to post comments and questions about publicly-held companies. A couple of the major ones are at Yahoo! (www.yahoo.com, search under Finance, look up a company's stock quote, and click on "Messages") and Raging Bull (www.ragingbull.com). My feeling about message boards is that, despite much of the drivel that passes for information ("This stock's going to rock . . . I feel great . . . "), they provide a sense of how investors feel about a particular company. Obviously, investors are going to be happier about a company whose stock is going up than about one whose stock is going down. But beyond that, you can ferret out particular complaints and questions—about the pace of product development, for instance, or about a company's promotional efforts. And occasionally, you'll discover tidbits of important information—about a key executive hire or about a revealing article in a local newspaper.

■ *Investment publications.* There are hundreds of investment magazines, newspapers, newsletters, and online sites devoted to keeping track of publicly-held companies. These range from *The Wall Street Journal* and *Investor's Business Daily* to *Money* and *Worth* magazines to *Red Herring* to the Motley Fool (www.motleyfool.com) and Hoover's (www.hoovers.com) Web sites. Many of these are searchable by company, so you can read all the articles a particular publication or site has run or stored on a specific organization.

Putting It All Together

If you approach the data-gathering process seriously, you'll likely find yourself before long with a huge amount of information. More than likely, you'll have more from your search of public companies than of private companies, but in either case, you may feel overwhelmed. Here are a few tips for making the most of your data:

■ *Know when to stop.* How do you know you've obtained everything you need? One sure sign that you've got most of what you're going to get is when you begin to see important items repeating themselves. It may be the news about an upcoming product, or the appointment of a new executive, or the existence of a lawsuit. The fact that the new articles or documents you are uncovering are going over similar ground is a strong indication that any additional investigative efforts on your part won't be as productive as previous ones. However, you may want to continue your hunt in this situation if there is some specific piece of information that you very much want but haven't been able to locate—such as the career background of the company's president or information about the company's competitors.

130

■ *Be on the lookout for inaccurate or conflicting data.* The good news about the Internet is that it provides us with access to more data than we ever could hope to fully access. The bad news is that more of that data is inaccurate than we probably want to know. For one thing, the media make many errors—many more than are ever acknowledged in their own "corrections" sections. Names of executives are misspelled, products are inaccurately described, and quotes are taken out of context. And data services like D&B disseminate the inaccurate information that companies provide. One way to counteract this problem is to get as close in your investigating to the original source as possible—official company documents, court testimony, and account executives of suppliers who work with your target company. In addition, you should be alert to conflicting information. If you see a key product described in significantly different ways by two business publications, you should try to determine which is accurate, or whether they're both off. The best way to do this is to keep a list of such discrepancies and to ask your target company contact about them. Listen for the answers and explanations— whether there really is confusion or a reporter has just misreported the data.

■ *Be alert to the "hidden agendas" of commentators.* You may have heard it said that everyone seems to have an axe to grind. That is often the case with industry experts, analysts, mutual fund managers, and others that the media quote about the prospects of particular companies. Their optimistic comments about a company often stem from the fact that they've invested in it and want to see its price head up. You won't be able to determine everyone's hidden agenda as you do your research, but you should keep a skeptical eye to the comments being made about your target company.

In sum, the Internet has made it harder than ever for companies to hide important information. Your challenge is

131

to make sure you find what you need to make an informed decision. ■

Chapter 11

Tricks of the Trade: How Owners Stretch Their Options

It's not that employers are trying to be devious—it's just that the fewer shares they make available to you, the more are available to the owners. So they may try to build up the potential value of the stock, make the vesting periods stretch far into the future or fail to allow for automatic vesting in certain key situations. Learn the details of five of the most common tricks, and what you can do to circumvent them.

E mployers sometimes take advantage of the fact that employees are naive about stock options. Consider this story from an owner of a technology company, published in *Fast Company* magazine in 1996:

The owner offered a key engineering candidate options for 50,000 shares of his company's stock. The employee refused, saying he wouldn't settle for anything less than 100,000 shares—the number his friend had received at another company. The owner advised the engineer that the other company had twice as many shares outstanding, so the effective number of shares was the same. Nothing doing. The engineer had to have 100,000 shares.

So the entrepreneur came up with a solution. He declared a stock split that quadrupled the number of shares outstanding, and then gave the employee the options on

133

100,000 shares. The employee was thrilled to have achieved his goal. The entrepreneur could only shake his head in wonderment that the employee never bothered to determine that he wound up with only half the actual ownership that he would have achieved originally. In other words, if the stock was worth $2 a share before the split, the 50,000 shares would have had a value of $100,000. After the quadrupling of shares, the same stock would have been worth 50 cents a share, making 100,000 shares worth $50,000.

I guess you could call that a win-win situation, since both the employee and employer are happy. But it's really a loss for the employee and a gain for the owner.

It's important to keep in mind that owners who hand out stock options are really taking stock from themselves and giving it to employees. That's the way I looked at it as a company owner. As employees gained options in our company, my ownership stake was potentially declining (assuming the employees actually exercised the shares). That realization can drive owners to, shall we say, manipulate certain aspects of stock ownership to their advantage.

I don't want to suggest that there is anything dishonest going on here. And I'd venture from the owners I've known that most don't begrudge employees the potential stock ownership they are receiving via options. So the "tricks" I describe here aren't necessarily mean-spirited in intent.

Five Common "Tricks"

As I discussed in Chapter 2, owners are handing out more stock these days, in significant measure because the competition for good people is so intense. The owners also want the stock to serve as an incentive, increasing company valuation to everyone's benefit. But that doesn't mean they always like doing it.

Here are some "tricks of the trade" to be aware of as you negotiate for and obtain options, especially in smaller private companies, where the opportunities for sleight of hand are greatest.

1. *Overstating the opportunity.* The most common "trick" is to overstate the likely value of the stock you will be receiving options for and the timing of an IPO. Especially in the unprecedented stock market we've experienced over the past five years, it's easy for owners to cite instances of amazing advances. If a privately-held online auction company is trying to recruit you, the owner might say, "You saw what happened with eBay's and Priceline's stocks after they went public. Everyone who had options became a multimillionaire." Keep in mind that most of the online auction companies that followed haven't necessarily done as well. In addition, going public isn't a trivial matter. An owner who says his company is going public "within a year" could well be exaggerating. It can take six months or longer to arrange an offering once an investment banker is onboard. A company must usually be able to demonstrate rapidly-rising revenues, a super-duper patent, or some other evidence of significant value before investment bankers will want to be involved in an IPO. If a company says it plans to go public within a few months, ask for the name of its investment banker. If that name isn't forthcoming, be suspicious.

2. *Stretching the vesting.* The longer it takes for your options to "vest"—that is, become available for you to purchase at the option price—the longer you'll have to hang around to actually obtain stock. Vesting usually happens over a period of three to five years. With three-year vesting, you can, after years one through three, purchase one-third of your options, while with five-year vesting, it's one-fifth of your options after years one through five. (In some cases, you can be exercising options on a quarterly basis after the first year's vesting.) In today's job and stock markets,

135

however, five years is a long time. If anything, the trend today is toward shorter vesting periods; some companies allow all options to be exercised after a year. A company that has a five-year vesting period is, to my way of thinking, sending a message that it's going to hold onto its stock as long as it possibly can. If you're serious about maximizing wealth via options, I'd be careful about getting involved with a company that has five-year vesting.

3. *Creating new classes of stock.* This is a little trick that some owners pull, not so much to make life difficult for option holders, but in order to obtain financing. Here's the deal: The options you receive are invariably for shares of *common stock*. However, some companies issue new classes of stock to private investors like venture capital firms, which insist on the special stock as a condition of making the investment. As noted in Chapter 2, these new classes of stock are usually referred to as *preferred stock.*

As the name suggests, preferred stock really is "preferred" in important ways—for example, preferred stockholders may have certain rights not available to common stockholders, such as to approve certain kinds of transactions or to elect a certain number of directors. Their most critical rights may come into play if the company encounters financial problems. Thus, if the company is sold in "fire sale" circumstances, proceeds will go first to holders of preferred stock—possibly enough to repay their investment, plus a guaranteed rate of return—and secondarily to common stockholders. But if there's nothing left after the preferred shareholders have received their cash allotments, well, too bad for the common shareholders. I have a friend who had options in a technology company that received many millions of dollars of investment from venture capitalists. The company didn't quite perform up to expectations, so the board decided to sell it. The venture capitalists received preferred stock, and when all was said and done, my friend received a few thousand dollars for his option shares—a huge disappointment given the fact that he joined the company at its start and was there for four years. I've been in a similar situation, watching a fast-growing Internet company that granted me options (in exchange for consulting I provided, and which I've since exercised) hand out new preferred shares (Series A, B, C, D, E, etc.) to various groups of investors over the last few years; the only hope I have for realizing value as an owner of common stock is that the company goes public or is acquired for a large multiple of its sales, in which case the preferred shares will be converted into common shares, and everyone will be happy.

4. *Failing to allow automatic vesting if there's an acquisition or public offering.* Most employees who receive stock options fantasize about getting rich via an IPO. But it's also possible for stock options to pay off big-time if your company is acquired—provided that its stock option agreement provides for automatic vesting in that circumstance. Thus, you could be granted 50,000 stock options that vest over four years by a young private company, and after 23 months see the company acquired by a large corporation for, say, $2 a share. Aha, you think, $100,000 of instant cash (minus the $5,000 purchase price, assuming a 10-cents-a-share option price). Not so fast if the stock option agreement doesn't allow for automatic vesting in the event of an acquisition. In that situation, you're only entitled to what's already vested—in our hypothetical situation, 12,500 shares, worth $25,000. A big letdown, considering you've been with the company nearly two years. But it is a slick way for owners to hold onto more of the stock than they might. When we put together the stock option agreement for our company, we intentionally included a provision for automatic vesting in the event of an acquisition, and our employees were grateful when the acquisition actually occurred at the end of 1999. But we were told by our lawyers that we were in the minority of private companies.

5. *Changing the rules.* As companies become more experienced, they are also becoming shrewder in their treatment of options. Increasingly, they are adjusting their options programs to try and make sure that options serve their original purposes of motivation and "golden handcuffs." And increasingly, these adjustments favor the company, and penalize the employee. One example of an adjustment is something known as "clawback" provisions in option plans, as described in a *Fortune* article of April 17, 2000. The clawback provisions may provide that you forfeit all your options, vested or not, if you are fired. If you resign, you may lose the opportunity to exercise vested options the day you leave rather than the customary 90 days later. And sometimes you lose your exercise rights, or even your profits from exercising the options, if you go to work for a competitor.

Protecting Yourself

All of the tricks just described have either of two potential effects:

1. Getting you to join the company through what might be considered false pretenses.

2. Getting you to take fewer options than you might otherwise have accepted.

The best way to protect yourself is to get your hands on as much stock as possible as quickly as possible. You do that by maximizing the number of shares you are entitled to and reducing the vesting period as much as possible. Previous chapters have discussed ways to maximize the number of shares you receive. But how do you speed up your access to the shares? Generally speaking, by finding out about possible pitfalls, like the absence of automatic vesting in the event of an acquisition. In addition, you may want to try to negotiate some special privileges for yourself. Here are some questions to consider in order to ensure that you actually gain access to the shares you've negotiated in as brief a period as possible:

How do I get around a long vesting period? You'd really hate to let a five-year vesting period prevent you from taking that dream job with a fast-growing private company that looks as if it could go public in a year. Especially if that's the one concern that's come up, and it's come up at the very end of the hiring process. When you bring it up, the company's owners may suggest that they can't do anything about it, because of "company policies." But as we all know, company policies are made to be changed, and there's nothing that says the company can't shorten your vesting period and/or increase the total number of shares you have options for, to increase the number that you can acquire each year, in consideration of the absence of automatic vesting. Your success in obtaining special treatment will be governed by your negotiating leverage. That is, the more the company wants you, the easier time you'll have gaining more shares or an agreement to shorten the vesting period.

How many classes of stock are there? Most private companies in their early stages have only one class of stock, and it's common stock. It's when the venture capitalists begin getting involved that preferred stock begins to appear. Because preferred stock is usually issued at the behest of the venture capitalists, it's not something that you as an employee can influence a great deal. However, if you are joining a company that is venture funded and has preferred stock, you can negotiate for a larger number of options than you might otherwise take. The reasoning is simple: The existence of preferred shares increases the risk that you'll eventually be cut out of some or all of the acquisition proceeds you might have received if all shareholders were treated equally. The owner will tell you that when the company is wildly successful and goes public or is acquired, all the preferred stock will be converted back into common stock. While that may occur, the final decision will depend on which course makes the preferred shareholders come out better financially, and common stockholders have no say in the matter.

Is there automatic vesting in the event of an acquisition? A negative answer to this should give you pause about the overall company, since it suggests that the owners are trying to avoid making available all the options to which they have committed. Business owners might argue that providing automatic vesting takes away incentive from employees after an acquisition is completed. But this assumes that the acquiring company is amenable to adapting your company's option program into one of its own, and continuing option and vesting provisions you had as part of its own program—a fairly optimistic assumption. Once acquisitions are complete, prior arrangements tend to be forgotten in the confusion of trying to assimilate the acquired company. So you're not out of bounds to argue that you want to be protected before an acquisition and, if you can't be protected with automatic vesting, then you want a larger number of shares—perhaps 25% to 50% more—in consideration. Then, you can properly argue, you can feel comfortable about simply transitioning to an acquiring company, and the new methods it will likely implement (perhaps including issuing its own options) to retain and incentivize employees from acquired companies.

Is there any "fine print" I should be aware of? In particular, you want to know what provisions exist for exercising vested options if you leave the company. Would they have to be exercised immediately, or might you have 30 or 90 days after departing the company? Also, you want to know if there are any special circumstances under which additional options might be made available, such as the company exceeding its earnings expectations.

In addition, you should request some time to review the offer letter you receive, with particular attention to its terminology about stock options. If you're puzzled about anything, and do not receive what you consider to be clear enough responses from the company, feel free to show the letter to a lawyer.

If you're still in doubt about the situation, ask to look at the company's stock option agreement. The company is under no obligation to share it with you, and officials will likely be surprised that you are asking for it. Chances are it won't provide a lot of information you don't already have, but it might be reassuring that you haven't overlooked anything.

Keep in mind that in any such major decision, the end result won't be crystal clear. There will likely be plusses and minuses. Your challenge will be to keep an eye on the big picture. So long as there's nothing seriously problematic, and you like the overall job and company situation, you should go with your gut. But a series of problems around stock options may be a tip-off to more serious company issues lurking beneath the surface. ■

Chapter 12

The Tax Consequences of Equity Compensation
(Warning: They Can Be Very Serious)

Imagine exercising options and then having to borrow money to pay taxes on profits from stock you can't even sell. Believe it or not, an acquisition of your company can put you in a financial squeeze rather than make you rich. What are the most dangerous scenarios lurking on the horizon? How do you negotiate in advance to avoid such scenarios? What strategies are there to minimize your taxes? Here's how to keep Uncle Sam from springing an unpleasant surprise on you.

I magine this situation: You recently joined what you think is a hot dot-com company. As part of your employment package, you were granted options on 20,000 shares, at 10 cents a share. One day, a couple of months into your tenure—just after you've finally gotten business cards and your own e-mail address—the company's president calls everyone together with "a very exciting announcement." It turns out that your dot-com has just been acquired by a larger dot-com for cash and stock totaling $2 a share. And, yes, he adds, your company's stock option plan provides for immediate vesting in the event of an acquisition.

"Wow!" you think. That's a $38,000 bonus ($40,000 in current value, minus the $2,000 cost of the stock, at 10 cents a share), in only two months. Hey, this stock option business is pretty cool!

You float back to your desk, your mind far from the office. You're already planning that trip to an ashram in India you've long fantasized about visiting. And there's the home entertainment center you've long wanted to set up in your condo. You've just launched into a Web search under "ashram" and "India" when the company's chief financial officer taps you on the shoulder. He wants to meet with you and a handful of other company newbies.

There are some tax issues associated with this merger that you need to be aware of, he tells you. He looks grim as he continues on. You remember the president saying the deal was for cash and stock? Well, one-fourth of the acquisition price is in cash and three-fourths is in stock of the acquiring company. So, you begin calculating in your mind, you'll be netting $8,000 cash ($10,000 minus the $2,000 purchase price of your company's shares), plus $30,000 worth of stock in the acquiring company. You'll sell the new company's stock and . . . what's the big deal?

"You also need to be aware," the CFO says, "that the merger deal prohibits any of us from selling our stock for at least a year. This is pretty standard." Well, you think, at least there'll be enough cash for the ashram trip; the entertainment center will just have to be put off a year.

The CFO isn't done yet, though. "The real reason" he called you newbies together, he explains, is that because of "tax rules," your entire gain must be treated as if it were salary. In fact, your company is required to immediately deduct all withholding taxes—federal and state income taxes, FICA (Social Security), and so on and so forth. "For most of you, that will be about 40% of the gain."

Another employee raises his hand. "You aren't suggesting that we have to pay taxes on stock, when we can't sell the stock for a year."

The CFO clears his throat and looks down at his shoes. "Yes, that's exactly what I'm suggesting. The company will take it out of your next paycheck as part of withholding. And if the cash portion of the acquisition price isn't enough, the taxes will come out of your wages. And if your wages during the next pay period aren't enough to cover the taxes, they'll come out of your wages during the pay period after that. Just remember, these aren't my rules, these are IRS rules, which the company's law firm has investigated very thoroughly. This wasn't our intention for the stock option plan."

You're continuing to calculate in your mind. Forty percent of $38,000—why that comes out to more than $15,000! That means you'll be paying *in* $7,000 (on top of the $8,000 net cash proceeds) to complete this transaction. That's almost two months of pay, based on your salary of $4,000 a month. No pay for almost two months! You have $5,000 in the bank. You may have to borrow $2,000 from your parents.

The CFO is speaking again. "Just keep in mind that we have high expectations for the stock you'll receive. We think it's going to appreciate substantially over the next year or two, or we wouldn't have done this deal."

Big f...g deal, you're thinking. I'll go broke to make this deal happen. And this is a windfall?

As incredible as this story may seem, it is actually based on a real one involving a business acquaintance of mine who sold his Internet company. Although the actual numbers differed, he had to break this same news to his newest employees, and they were as shocked as you'd expect.

This story underscores the title of this chapter—the tax consequences associated with equity compensation can be very serious, indeed. This chapter is devoted to explaining

145

the key tax ramifications associated with equity compensation.

The Harsh Reality

The day you're able to cash in your stock options is supposed to be a happy one. You'd think that, so long as the stock is worth more than the option price, it would be a happy day. In many cases, it is a happy day. But the harsh reality is that, no matter what happens on that day, the Tax Man will be there with his hand out.

The challenge facing you as you obtain stock options is to anticipate as much as possible the ramifications of the Tax Man's presence. Here is a range of common equity compensation situations, from the most favorable to the least favorable. The least favorable includes an explanation of how the circumstances described in the opening example of this chapter could come to be. Be aware that these situations are far from all-inclusive. In addition to being serious, the tax consequences associated with equity compensation are extremely complex, to the extent that so-called tax experts sometimes disagree about what's appropriate and legal. Indeed, the tax laws around options are a clear illustration of why our country's tax laws need to be simplified (end of political lecture). With that proviso, be forewarned that you should consult with your own accountant or tax advisor about the tax implications associated with your equity compensation situation.

Four Common Tax Situations

1. *You purchase stock under your incentive stock option plan and hold it for more than a year.* In this situation, you exercise your options at least a year in advance of when you expect to sell the stock. Then, when you sell the stock, your gain is a long-term capital gain, taxable at the most favorable 20% rate maximum.

Here's an example of this situation: You joined a young private company's marketing group on Jan. 2, 1998, and received options to acquire 10,000 shares of stock at 10 cents a share. Under the company's four-year vesting provisions, you purchased all of the allowable 2,500 shares that vested after the first year, on Jan. 3, 1999, for $250.

In late 1999, the company went public at $30 a share. On Jan. 5, 2000, with the stock still at $30 a share, you sold your 2,500 shares, and received $75,000.

Ideally, you would have had a simple long-term gain in this transaction of $74,750, incurring a maximum federal tax of 20% on the $74,750 (or $14,950). I say ideally because there is a possibility that you could have been penalized by something referred to as "the bargain element" of the transaction—the difference in price between the original 10-cents-a-share price of the options in early 1998 and the value of the options when you exercised them in January 1999. *If* the company had changed the option price for *new* options granted in January 1999—say, to 50 cents a share—you might have had a different tax obligation for the difference between 10 cents and 50 cents, related to the Alternative Minimum Tax, which can be higher than the long-term capital gains tax even though this new option strike price doesn't affect the options that we are discussing. I'm not going to try to explore the implications of the Alternative Minimum Tax, because this is an entire tax subject unto itself, with the net effect differing from individual to individual. As I said, this stuff gets complicated, and you need to consult with a tax expert. If you live in a state that has an income tax, you may have a state tax obligation, though it will probably mimic the federal approach with a lower rate for long-term gains.

The key point here is that you receive the most favorable tax treatment overall if you are able to hold any stock you acquire via options for at least a year. The tax regulations also require that you acquired the stock at least one year after being granted the option (which is nearly always the case because of vesting provisions).

One other way you potentially benefit from holding your stock for more than a year: If your company is acquired by another company a year or more after you've bought your stock, say for cash and stock, you only pay taxes at the long-term capital gain rate on the cash portion; the gains on the stock of the acquiring company don't get taxed until you sell the stock, unlike the situation described in this chapter's opening example.

2. *You purchase stock under your incentive stock option plan and hold it for less than a year.* In this situation, you've taken the "show-me-the-cash" approach to options. You've exercised the options as soon as they've vested, and sold the stock as soon as possible to get your hands on the cash. Of course, in order for you to be able to play out this scenario, the company must be publicly held. If it is private, there is no market for the stock.

Using the example from the previous situation, here's how things might play out: You joined a young private company's marketing group on Jan. 2, 1998, and received options to acquire 10,000 shares of stock at 10 cents a share. Under the company's four-year vesting provisions, you purchased all of the allowable 2,500 shares that vested after the first year, on Jan. 3, 1999, for $250.

In late 1999, November 10 to be exact, the company went public at $30 a share. You immediately sold your 2,500 shares at that price, and received $75,000.

Because you held the stock for less than a year, your gain of $74,750 is treated as ordinary income, which means you pay federal and state taxes at your ordinary highest rate—usually 28% to 33%. And if you live in a state with an income tax, you will also likely pay a higher rate.

If your federal obligation is 33%, your tax will be about $29,000, or nearly $10,500 more than in the first situation. Thus, you can see that the tax differential between a long-term and short-term gain can be quite substantial. It therefore behooves you to hold onto the stock for more than a year if at all possible. If your company is in a highly unstable or dynamic industry sector, then this may not be desirable.

3. *You purchase stock via nonqualified stock options.* If you work for an established publicly-held company, the options you receive may be "nonqualified"— that is, not subject to the same tax protections as incentive stock options. The problem with nonqualified options is that you are required to pay ordinary income tax on the difference, or "spread," between the grant price and the stock's market value when you exercise your options. Even if you don't sell the stock after exercising the options, a problem arises because you have to pay cash to the IRS without receiving cash in hand. You will thus need to come up with the cash to pay required taxes if you decide you want to hold the stock for possible further gains.

The stock penalty can be significant. Consider this situation: You have options for 20,000 shares at 50 cents a share. At the end of your first year, 5,000 shares have vested, so you purchase them for $2,500. But let's say the shares are publicly trading at $2 a share, giving them a real value of $10,000. The difference between $2,500 and $10,000, or $7,500, is considered a gain that is taxable as ordinary income. Ouch. You have to pay the tax, even if you want to hold the stock. The situation is even worse if the company is privately held. Then, you could have the same circumstances and valuations I just described (with the stock valued at $2 a share based on the company's growth), except you can't even sell the stock to raise money for the taxes.

The only good news is that any subsequent appreciation in the stock is taxed based on when you sell the stock. If you hold it for more than a year, and it has risen further in price, you'll pay long-term capital gains taxes on the difference between the valuation when you exercised the option, and the new value.

The only other possible good tax news associated with nonqualified options is that companies get to deduct the "spread" on which you pay taxes at the time of exercising the option as a compensation expense. This may not directly benefit you as an employee, but it will help your company reduce its own taxes, and thus increase its own profitability.

4. *You receive what's deemed "a bargain" by the IRS.* This is the sledgehammer that some of the employees in this chapter's opening example encountered. The rules associated with it are spelled out in something known as Section 83 of the IRS code. I only mention it because lawyers and accountants sometimes refer to it as a Section 83 issue.

The problem comes up if your employer grants you options at a purchase price that everyone should have known was "a bargain." Thus, the employees who received options at 10 cents a share just a few months prior to the company's sale were getting a bargain, in the IRS' view, since the company had already entered into negotiations to sell the company, and had ample reason to believe that the stock's value was much closer to $2 a share than it was to 10 cents a share.

Under the IRS regulations, the entire gain becomes ordinary income for employees, subject to the same withholding provisions as regular wages. The real kicker comes when some of the proceeds for your stock are paid as stock, because the IRS treats the stock as if it were cash compensation. This makes it harder for you to find the cash to pay the taxes you owe.

Strategies: Position Yourself to Minimize Taxes

Clearly, taxes can take a lot of the fun out of stock options. When it comes to options, Uncle Sam has both hands open, set to rummage through your pockets and pick them cleaner than you ever could have imagined. Your challenge is to keep him at bay, and maximize the amount of money you keep from the stock you purchase via your options.

The strategy you adopt to fend off Uncle Sam will depend on your actual circumstance—the type of options you have, as well as possibly the company's situation.

■ *Incentive options—buy and hold.* If you truly believe in the future of your company and you're lucky enough to receive incentive stock options, which are handed out most widely among early-stage companies, your approach should be similar to that of long-term stock investors everywhere. That is, you want to acquire as much stock as possible and hold it for the long term. At a minimum, you want to hold your stock for at least a year so that, if it's appreciated in value and you want to sell it, you'll pay the lowest possible long-term capital gain rates on your profits. What this means in practice is that you should exercise all your options immediately as they vest, paying the option price for the shares and setting aside the stock. An additional benefit of this approach is that you put a lid on the "bargain element" of the stock that could continue adding up if you delay purchasing. One risk to this approach is that your company stays private and independent so that there's no "liquidity," or opportunity to sell. Another risk is that the stock goes down sharply during the year you are waiting to obtain favorable tax treatment; one way to handle this dilemma is to sell a quarter or half of the stock immediately, even though you'll be paying higher tax rates, to lock in some sure profits.

■ *Nonqualified options—delay exercising options.*
Here your strategy should in most cases be the opposite of
handling incentive stock options. Because you likely will
incur a short-term tax liability immediately upon purchasing
the stock, the idea is to wait as long as possible before
exercising your options and creating a tax event. In many
cases, you will have up to ten years from the issue date to
exercise your options (unless you leave the company, in
which case you'll probably only have three months following
your departure date to exercise the options), so you'll have an
opportunity to follow the company's performance and
determine if it's worth your while to purchase the stock. The
main exception to this advice would be if your company's
stock hasn't appreciated much from the option price, and you
expected a big advance in the near-term future. For example,
you might have options at 50 cents a share, and now that you
can exercise some, the company is still private, and the
valuation is 75 cents a share. Yet, you feel confident that an
initial public offering could happen within the next year or
two, which could make the stock worth $15 or $20 a share.
Then, it's worth the risk to pay immediate taxes on the 25-
cents-a-share gain you'd have when buying the stock, and set
yourself up to be in a long-term capital gain situation after
the company goes public.

■ *Something's a-brewing—go in with your eyes
wide open.* You may, during your job interviews and follow-
up investigation of a particular company, sense that a
possible acquisition or public offering is in the offing. You
may learn about the possibilities from remarks of employees
you meet, or from newspaper or magazine articles you read.
This can be very exciting, suggesting a big financial
opportunity. You just need to make sure you protect yourself
because, if you're dealing with an early-stage private
company, your possible tax penalties won't be at the top of
its agenda. So when you get to the matter of stock options as

part of your employment package, be sure to inquire about when the options' purchase price was last adjusted (i.e. from $0.10 to $0.50). If you learn that "it's been a while," you should speak up—say that you have a friend who was badly burned tax-wise by undervalued options in a company that was acquired. If the company won't investigate the situation with an eye to adjusting the options' value upward, reexamine whether you want to join the company. It could wind up being an expensive proposition.

Getting the Money You Need

It's easy for me to tell you to exercise options and lay out hard cash as soon as possible. But, you may have been asking along the way, how will you get the money you need to buy the stock—especially if you don't have a great deal of savings available?

Here are two possible approaches to acquiring stock without having the necessary cash on hand:

1. *Cashless exercise.* Many stock option plans provide for this vehicle, which allows you to use some of your stock in advance of actually buying it, or else to temporarily borrow from part of the proceeds of selling stock the money you need to exercise the remaining options. Here's a simple example of how it might work: You have the vested options that allow you to purchase 10,000 shares of stock at 10 cents a share, but the stock has a value of $1.00 a share. So you'd borrow $1,000 from a stockbroker with whom your company has a relationship, exercise your options, and immediately sell 1,000 of the shares to repay the broker, leaving you with 9,000 shares. You'd be subject to the same tax provisions as if you had simply purchased all the shares.

2. *Borrow the money.* If your company's plan doesn't allow for cashless exercise, you may want to explore ways of borrowing the money. While I don't ordinarily encourage individuals to borrow from relatives or to take out home equity loans, in the case of exercising stock options, I feel more comfortable making such recommendations. This is especially the case if the company is about to go public or already is public. If you're dealing with a publicly-held company, you can always sell part of the stock to repay the loan if you feel compelled to dispense with the debt right away. But if you can afford to pay off the loan over a five- or ten-year period, this approach can be very worthwhile. Another borrowing approach includes taking a loan against life insurance you own. Unless you feel very positive about the prospects of your company's stock, I'd caution against more costly and risky borrowing sources, such as using credit cards, since the interest rates can be quite high, even if they start out low via introductory rates. Remember, in addition to having to repay any loans you take out, you may well have to fork over money to the IRS. ■

Chapter 13

Making the Most of Your Opportunities: Strategies for Managing and Growing Equity Incentives

*The last thing you want to do is to treat your stock options
like lottery tickets, stashing them away and forgetting about
them. They're an investment that can become valuable.
Learn how to manage them like a stock portfolio. For
example, what do you do if their value plummets? Do you
know where to find additional stock option opportunities?
There's no reason why you can't establish a portfolio, just
like the professionals.*

A premise of this book is that equity incentives are really an investment, as opposed to a crapshoot or lottery. As such, equity incentives need to be "managed," much as you might manage your stock market portfolio, budget, or taxes. This means monitoring the details of what's going on and making adjustments as you move through the process of accumulating options and other incentives and converting them into stock—what your holdings are; how the value is changing; what the vesting, expiration, and other key dates are; and so forth. And periodically, you try to take a big-

155

picture view and perhaps adjust your overall approach to
handling your equity incentives.

There are really two aspects, then, to managing
equity incentives:

1. Keeping track of what you have so you can make
wise decisions about how much stock to accumulate in a
particular company.

2. Developing an overall strategy with respect to
equity incentives in terms of what you want to accomplish
from an investment perspective—for example, maximize
your holdings in one or two companies or assemble a
portfolio of several companies.

Monitoring What You Have

Unfortunately, there's a tendency to treat stock
options and other equity incentive documents much the same
as lottery tickets—to bury them away somewhere and forget
about them. This can be dangerous if the stock options
eventually come to be worth something.

At the Internet company I helped found, several
members of our five-person board of advisors, who all held
stock and/or options in the company, couldn't locate their
certificates and agreements when the company was sold.
They needed their documentation to receive their share of the
proceeds from the acquiring company. Fortunately, our
lawyers were able to provide these individuals with
substitute documents. In one case, though, a board member
actually misplaced one of the substitute documents, which
then had to be re-created!

The fact that we kept after these individuals certainly
made it easier for them. Had we been involved in a different
kind of transaction (one not requiring that all shareholders
tender their stock and options), they might have forfeited
their rights to compensation in that particular transaction by

156

ignoring the mailings sent out to all shareholders and option holders.

My point here is that equity incentives should be treated as valuable investments, whether or not they actually have significant value today. Presumably you accept them in return for your time and skills, and with the expectation that they will become valuable.

Here are some of the key issues and decisions around making the most of equity incentives:

■ *Know what you're entitled to and when.* Keep tabs on your vesting and expiration dates, in particular. You don't want to turn a long-term capital gain into a short-term one because you inadvertently waited longer than necessary to exercise incentive stock options. Remember that the sooner you exercise your options, the easier it will be to hold them for more than one year, thus reducing your tax exposure. And you definitely don't want options to expire before you've decided whether to exercise them—just because you lost track of the expiration date. One way to keep track of your options is to enter key dates into your Palm Pilot or other electronic datebook, or to enter them into investment software you use. You can even use an online reminder service, usually used for birthdays and anniversaries, to let you know about key option dates.

■ *Be absolutely certain about any decision not to exercise the full amount of options.* In other words, don't let any temporary cash shortfalls deter you from obtaining all the stock you possibly can. Obviously, if the value of your company's stock is below the strike price, you'll likely want to put off exercising options. But generally speaking, if your option price is below what the share price is (or seems to be, if it's a private company), try to acquire as much stock as you can, even if you have to forego purchase of a new "toy" like a car, or borrow from relatives. Once again, keep in mind that you got involved with the company in significant

157

measure because you saw a big opportunity to capitalize on its rising value. Don't let that opportunity slip away.

■ *Be prepared to accept additional equity opportunities in lieu of a raise.* For most companies, especially fast-growing ones, it's much easier to give away stock options than cash. If you're in a company that's growing quickly because it is experiencing marketplace success, you may want to make salary review time a time to push for an increase in options. I know of a marketing manager in a fast-growing, publicly-held Internet company who got bogged down with upper management in a bitter argument because her salary review provided her with a $10,000 annual raise when she thought she should be getting a $20,000 raise. She completely lost sight of the fact that the stock she purchased via options a year earlier had increased in value by $94,000 during that time. She really had achieved much more than a cash raise could possibly provide. One way she might have extended her cash raise, and defused the argument, was to give in on the cash portion and push instead for an extra 20% or 25% of stock options.

■ *Take your options opportunities into account when changing jobs.* There's a custom among investment banking executives to jump ship in January, just after receiving their year-end bonuses, which are often quite substantial. This mindset can be applied to equity incentives. If you're thinking of changing jobs, try to do it just after you've passed a vesting milestone, rather than a month or two before potentially valuable options vest. Of course, timing such matters so conveniently isn't always possible, or even advisable. Job opportunities have a way of opening up at inopportune times, and you may not have the luxury of putting a suitor on hold for a month or two so that you can complete a vesting period. But at least consider as part of your overall list of job pros and cons your stock incentive situation. Additionally, you could use a pending vesting

opportunity in your existing job ("Gee, I'm going to be
walking away from a $40,000 windfall due me next month.")
as a way to get your new employer to increase your salary
and options, and maybe even to grant a signing bonus.
Remember: everything is negotiable.

■ *Try to help right a tilting situation.* No matter
how promising the company you are working for, there will
be bumps along the growth path, some of which could affect
the value of its equity. It could be the loss of a major
customer, or a key executive. The last thing you want to do
is bail out on your equity at the first sign of trouble with your
employer. Indeed, this is often the time when everyone in a
company needs to pitch in even more than usual to make
things right. If everyone rushes for the exits, then you can be
sure that your options or equity holdings won't have
significant future value—which leads to the next two points.

■ *Consider seeking additional options if your
company's stock plummets.* While you're trying to help right
a tilting situation, you should also consider whether to
request additional options. Going in for a raise when a
company's stock is down might seem to be in bad taste, but if
you position it correctly, you can pull it off—something like,
"Hey, I know we're having some problems, but I want you to
know that I still believe in this company. Just to let you
know how strongly I believe in the company, I'd like to
request some additional stock options, in lieu of the raise I
was considering asking for. Options won't cost the company
any cash out of pocket, and they'll go a long way toward
keeping me motivated."

■ *Be prepared to change jobs if your company's
value deteriorates badly.* If you joined a company and took
stock options in significant measure because you believed
you'd become wealthy, then you shouldn't feel terrible about
bailing out if things continue for a significant period of time
to move in the opposite direction. The situation isn't unlike

that involving an ordinary stock investment. If a stock performs poorly over a long period of time (at least six months), and you see little hope for a turnaround, then the logical thing to do is to sell the stock. So it is with stock options. If your investment isn't performing as expected, and shows no sign of righting itself, consider moving on to another one that shows more potential.

Developing a Portfolio Strategy

Building on the last point of the previous section, there's no rule that says you can't have equity incentives in more than one company. In fact, it can be argued that gaining access to equity in several companies is highly desirable, since you inevitably increase your risk by having too high a percentage of your assets in one investment. Increasingly, forward-thinking individuals and companies are beginning to understand this premise, and are focusing on accumulating options and stock in promising small companies. Consider the following examples:

■ Bob Shea, a Massachusetts computer systems expert who has worked as both an employee and a consultant with a number of small companies, has received stock options in four companies as part of his compensation over the last ten years. Three of the companies have gone public and one has been acquired, enabling him to earn some tidy windfalls in the process.

■ Jeffrey Shuman, a professor of entrepreneurship at Bentley College in Waltham, MA, has taken warrants (a cousin of stock options often used by professional investors, giving holders the right to buy stock at a certain price) in a dozen-and-a-half Internet companies as part of arrangements to provide consulting services to and be an advisory board member of the companies.

■ Michael Gonnerman, a Massachusetts financial consultant, has served on the boards of directors or advisory

160

boards of seven companies over the last nine years, and received stock or options from each company. The stock in each of the seven companies eventually paid off when the companies went public or were sold, yielding income more than two times his total seven-figure income over the nine years of consulting.

■ Heidrick & Struggles, a Chicago-based executive search firm, commonly receives equity as part of its compensation on searches it completes. By the beginning of 2000, it had equity stakes in more than 70 companies, and commitments for equity in another 200 searches, according to the Jan. 25, 2000, *New York Times.* The value of its warrants in just one of the companies, which had gone public, was in excess of $22 million.

■ Western Trading, a New York advertising agency, is obtaining "equity stakes from a carefully selected handful of Internet startups," according to *The Wall Street Journal* of Feb. 8, 2000. In return, the agency is assigning the companies its best talent and advertising space.

There are several messages here, prime among them that equity incentives are increasingly being used as a powerful currency that can gain promising companies access to talent and services they might not otherwise be able to obtain. More significant from the perspective of your situation, equity incentives are increasingly being used by recipient individuals and companies to accomplish a number of goals, including the following:

■ *Amass a portfolio.* Few smart investors hold just one or two stocks. Individuals who are savvy about it can use their equity incentives to put together a portfolio of companies, something on the order of what wealthy private investors and venture capitalists do.

■ *Get into promising companies ahead of the crowds.* Not only can ordinary individuals amass a portfolio, they can do it with companies that they wouldn't ordinarily get an opportunity to invest in. Typically, only wealthy investors and venture capitalists who had the means to invest $500,000 or more at a pop could gain access to promising young privately-held companies. Now working professionals and other individuals who are willing to invest their time and expertise can gain the same opportunities.

■ ***Diversifying your holdings.*** One of the dangers associated with obtaining stock options in a single company is just that—your opportunities are limited to what happens in one company over which you don't have extensive control. Even if its value increases significantly, the bulk of your investments are effectively tied up in one company. Of course, this isn't necessarily a bad problem to have—until the time comes that lightning strikes your company and a delayed product introduction or reduced earnings causes its stock to fall 25% or 30% in a day (as happens with increasing frequency in today's volatile markets). By obtaining options or other equity incentives in several companies, you effectively diversify your holdings and reduce overall risk. You aren't dependent on the outcome of one investment, and are thus less exposed to sharp swings in the value of your portfolio.

■ ***Increase the odds of becoming wealthy.*** This is a benefit related to the previous one. Diversification helps reduce the dangers associated with having too much of your assets tied up in a single company. It also increases your chances of becoming wealthy by spreading your "bets" among several entrants. Generally speaking, there are one or two great performers within a portfolio that create significant wealth; you improve your odds of hitting the right one or two as you diversify your holdings. To increase the odds of becoming wealthy, learn to think like an investor.

Learning to Think Like an Investor

How do you amass a portfolio of highly promising stock options or other equity incentives? Certainly being in the position of providing services that are highly valued by fast-growth companies is one way. Headhunters, corporate lawyers, accountants, and consultants are all in excellent positions to accumulate stock options. Increasingly, though, building contractors, office building owners who rent to small companies, and even restaurant owners who provide late-night meals to entrepreneurs and their employees are getting in on the act, offering to take stock or options in lieu of scarce cash.

Certainly individuals who are willing to change option-producing jobs every few years are in a position to assemble a portfolio over the course of a decade or so. But, as I noted earlier in this book, such an approach may conflict with career aspirations.

The bulk of what I discuss in this section applies to providers of professional services and individual contractors—individuals who can take on a number of clients at any one time, and thus pick and choose equity-yielding situations that most appeal to them. It's important to tread carefully in this arena, however. Professional investors like venture capitalists succeed as much by avoiding dry holes as they do by hitting it right. Here are some guidelines to make sure you don't trip on your own shoelaces:

■ *Be discriminating.* A savvy business associate of mine was loathe to accept equity incentives for consulting work because, in his experience, "You can wind up papering your walls with the stock certificates you receive." In other words, try not to get caught up in all the stock market hype going on around you, and remember that not only do most young companies never succeed in a big way, but that even when they do, the success can be a long time in coming. This means you need to examine very carefully any company in which you might be tempted to accept equity incentives— using the procedures described in Chapter 10 to obtain the information you need to make a smart decision.

■ *Forego only the cash you can afford to live without.* A public relations consultant in Atlanta learned this lesson the hard way when she accepted stock options in a company in exchange for her professional services. According to *The New York Times* of Feb. 27, 2000, she sacrificed part of her $150 per hour fee in exchange for stock options. She became frustrated, though, when her cash flow suffered, and the realization dawned that any payout from the options was far off in the future.

■ *Never take mostly stock unless you directly control its value and liquidity.* Sometimes cash-short entrepreneurs will be amenable to paying for most or all of the services they receive in stock options. As promising as a company might appear, accepting most or all of your compensation in stock has a tendency to demean the services you are providing. The reality is that most entrepreneurs still value cash the most. The only exception to this rule is a situation in which your duties affect the value and liquidity of the stock. One example involves a consultant brought in to help sell a company. When our company was ready to find an acquirer, we engaged a consultant to help negotiate the transaction. He was willing to accept the majority of his compensation in stock because he knew he'd have a major role in completing the transaction—and thereby determining the timing of the deal, and the value of his stock.

■ *Anticipate potential conflicts of interest.* It's important for professionals, in particular, to look further down the road from actually obtaining equity or options from a client. Yes, having a stake in the company should encourage you to work harder and be more creative. But what happens if a competitor to one of your holdings (and a

164

potential client) walks in the door and wants to do the same kind of deal? Does this relationship with Company A prevent you from working with Company B? What if Company B is willing to pay you more in cash and options than Company A? What happens if the company whose stock you hold doesn't perform as anticipated—do you continue providing services at lower or preferred rates based on having received the equity? None of these is an insurmountable problem, but each should be thought through.

Looking Ahead: Developing Your Own Personal Strategy

Sometimes, when you look at the business shelves of bookstores or in the business sections of magazines, you get the feeling that everyone wants to start a business and be like Bill Gates or Michael Dell. But the reality is that most people who start businesses don't have anywhere near the entrepreneurial talent of such individuals. And make no mistake about it, successful entrepreneurship is a talent.

I have increasingly come to believe that there's a strong argument to be made that assembling relatively small amounts of stock via options and other incentives in a collection of promising companies is a smarter and less risky way to accumulate wealth than starting your own business. Starting your own business, after all, necessitates putting all your eggs in one basket.

The key to success in establishing your own promising equity portfolio via incentives is twofold:

1. *Determine your own special talent.* To create the most attractive opportunities for yourself requires making yourself indispensable to some number of companies. The best way to do this is to identify what you are best at, and then go out and do it, and keep getting better at it. You also need to make sure that you effectively promote your expertise—by getting involved in trade and networking

organizations of other like-minded professionals so you get
the chance to talk yourself up, and learn about emerging
opportunities.

2. *Identify the teams that will succeed.* The more
opportunities you are exposed to, the more important it will
be for you to be selective. The best single indicator of
success, in my experience, is the talent and quality of the
individuals running a business. The savvier you can be in
judging these individuals, the better will be your chances of
signing on with the best company.

Get While the Getting's Good

What does the future hold for equity incentives?
While no one can say for sure, it seems reasonably safe to
expect that as long as the fundamental trends of a tight labor
market, a technological revolution, a fomenting entrepreneurial arena, and wide availability of investment capital
continue, then equity incentives will increase in importance.

Still and all, anytime something seems too good to be
true, it likely is. So it is likely to be with equity incentives,
especially stock options, which really have been better than
money for many individuals. Probably the biggest danger to
the use of equity incentives is a significant stock market
reversal, such as a major bear market (a sustained decline in
major markets of 20% or more). In that situation, the
valuations of many companies would decline below option
holders' strike prices. This would have the effect of putting a
damper on the IPO and acquisition markets, demoralizing
employees, and reducing the use of options.

No one knows when a bear market will strike. But
apart from that, we can likely expect to see a number of
significant changes over the next few years that may make
stock options, in particular, less attractive and/or widely
available. Here are some of the changes I foresee:

166

■ *Expect to see more official regulation of stock options.* A few years ago, the American Institute of Certified Public Accountants (AICPA), the standard-setting org-anization for the accounting profession, attempted to force companies to account for the financial impact of stock options on their income and balance sheets. Executives of technology companies, in particular, objected strenuously because breaking out the potential cost of options would have reduced earnings for many such companies. The AICPA eventually backed off, and now publicly-held companies need only note the expected impact of stock options in a footnote to their financial statements. But a number of economists and policy makers have expressed concern that stock options are really an inflationary force in our economy that companies should itemize as a cost. I would expect this issue to be raised again as stock options spread. If companies do have to more explicitly account for the impact of stock options, the companies will inevitably become less generous in handing them out.

■ *Expect the stock market to become more discriminating.* The last few years have seen record numbers of initial public offerings (IPOs), with many of them soaring 50% and more on the first day of trading. Much of that has had to do with the emergence of the Internet, and the public's unbridled optimism about valuing Internet stocks. That is already changing, though, as the markets begin to use the same criteria as with non-Internet companies—revenue, profits, marketplace prospects, and financial controls.

■ *Expect wider disparities in the awarding of options.* Just as many employees don't look very closely at the stock option component of compensation, neither do many companies. All that will likely change as both employees and employers increasingly come to appreciate the importance of options, and pay more attention to them in the course of hiring negotiations. Just as happens with

167

salaries, individuals in greatest demand will receive the largest grants of options, while those in less demand will receive much less.

■ *Expect more workers to demand a piece of the action.* Independent contractors who work exclusively for one company will increasingly expect to be included in on options. Already, a group of Microsoft independent contractors has sued that company for failing to be included in Microsoft's options program (just as Microsoft subcontractors have sued the company over other disparities between employees and independent contractors).

■ *Expect abuses to pop up.* I'm not sure exactly what will happen. But I do know that as an area of exciting profits comes on the scene, an unsavory element of schemers and crooks seems also to emerge. The best way to counteract abuses is knowledge, and hopefully this book will help in that regard.

There will likely be other effects, both positive and negative, of equity incentives. Their emergence signals a sea change in the workplace. Not only do they signal financial opportunity, but a whole new workplace democratization, especially in the wake of labor unions' decline. The wider availability of stock to employees and other stakeholders like professional service providers effectively gives them all a stake and a voice in more emerging companies.

Look for new employee voices to emerge at shareholder meetings. Look for new kinds of shareholder initiatives seeking changes in the workplace. And look for more lawsuits from employee stockholders. Aside from continuing to provide wealth-expanding opportunities, equity incentives will undoubtedly contribute to a whole new world of work. ■

Appendix A

Internet Resources

The World Wide Web offers a vast collection of resources to help you evaluate prospective employers, their prospects for growth, and their competitive positioning. You can also find salary statistics, tricks of the negotiating trade, recruitment sites, and much more. The following is just a sampling of the resources that you can find with the click of a mouse.

<u>Analyst/Industry-Research Firms</u>
Forrester Research
http://www.forrester.com/
GartnerGroup
http://gartner6.gartnerweb.com/public/static/home/home.html
Jupiter Communications
http://www.jup.com/home.jsp
META Group
http://www.metagroup.com/
The Yankee Group
http://www.yankeegroup.com/

<u>Career-Planning Resources</u>
Career Key
http://www2.ncsu.edu:8010/unity/lockers/users/l/lkj/
Keirsey Temperament Sorter
http://www.Keirsey.com

<u>Corporate Information</u>
Dun & Bradstreet
http://www.dnb.com
Standard & Poor's
http://www.standardandpoors.com/

EDGAR Database (SEC)
http://www.sec.gov/edaux/searches.htm

Financial Definitions
Campbell R. Harvey's Hypertextual Finance Glossary
http://www.duke.edu/~charvey/Classes/wpg/glossary.htm
Schaeffer's Investment Research
http://www.schaefersresearch.com

Investigative Resources:
Article and Industry Report Databases
Hoover's Online
http://www.hoovers.com
LEXIS-NEXIS
http://www.lexis-nexis.com/lncc/
Value Line
http://www.valueline.com/

Financial Service Sites
Bloomberg.com
http://www.bloomberg.com/
National Association of Securities Dealers
http://www.nasd.com/
New York Stock Exchange
http://www.nyse.com/
Quicken.com
http://www.quicken.com/
Reuters
http://www.reuters.com/

Online Newpapers & Magazines:
Business 2.0
http://www.business2.com/
BusinessWeek Online
http://www.businessweek.com/
CNET.com
http://www.cnet.com/
dowjones.com

http://dowjones.wsj.com/p/main.html
FORTUNE.com
http://www.fortune.com/
InformationWeek Online
http://www.informationweek.com/
Inter@ctive Week Online
http://www.zdnet.com/intweek/
INTERNETWEEK Online
http://www.internetwk.com/
Network Computing
http://www.networkcomputing.com/
The New York Times
http://www.nytimes.com/
TheStandard.com
http://www.thestandard.com/
TheStreet.com
http://www.thestreet.com
UpsideToday
http://www.upside.com/
The Wall Street Journal
http://www.wsj.com/

Negotiation Resources
Monster Mid-Career
http://midcareer.monster.com/experts/negotiation/

Online Job Postings
America's Career InfoNet
http://www.acinet.org/acinet/
CareerBuilder
http://www.careerbuilder.com/
CareerCity
http://www.careercity.com/
careerhunters.com
http://www.careerhunters.com/
CareerMosaic
http://www.careermosaic.com/
CareerPath.com
http://www.careerpath.com/service/cp/EndUser/Homepage

careers.wsj.com
http://www.careers.wsj.com/
Cruel World (Career Central)
http://www.cruelworld.com/index.asp
HotJobs.com
http://www.hotjobs.com/
Monster.com
http://www.monster.com
NationJob Network
http://www.nationjob.com/
Yahoo! Careers
http://careers.yahoo.com/

Patent Searches
US Patent and Trademark Office
http://www.uspto.gov/patft/

Salary Resources
Salary.com
http://www.salary.com/
Salary Source
http://www.salarysource.com/
WAGEWEB
http://www.wageweb.com/

Tax-Law Resources
Search IRS Database
http://192.239.92.40/search/index.html
IRS e-mail address
helpdesk@fedworld.gov
Attorney Locate
http://www.attorneylocate.com/
WEBLOCATOR
http://www.weblocator.com/

Valuation Resources
VentureLine
http://www.ventureline.com

Glossary

Above Water	Options allowing the purchase of shares of stock for less than the market price are said to be "above water."
Authorized Shares	The number of shares of stock available for a company to issue.
Bearish	Having a negative opinion about the future of the stock market.
Bullish	Having a positive opinion about the future of the stock market.
Capital Gains	The profit gained from the sale of an investment, such as stock, which is taxed at lower rates than ordinary income.
Cashless Exercise	Allows an individual to temporarily borrow the money needed to exercise options by selling some of his/her stock in order to cover the cost of the remaining shares.
Cliff Vesting	Allows option holders to exercise some or all of their options at once, such as after the first year of employment, instead of incrementally over a period of several quarters or years. (See Vesting Period.)
Common Stock	Ownership shares of a company entitling the holder to influence management decisions, and to share in corporate profits. In the event of bankruptcy or liquidation, common stockholders have a lower claim on corporate assets than do preferred stockholders.
Equity	Common stock in a company.
Exercise	The act of acquiring stock promised by an option.
Exercise Price	The price at which an option holder may buy shares of stock. Often referred to as the strike price.
Expire	Options are typically granted for a definite period of time. If individuals do not exercise the options before a specified date, they expire (meaning they are forfeited).
Forfeit	Employees forfeit or forego their right to exercise their options by leaving a company before all the options have vested—or by not exercising them

173

before their date of expiration because they are "under water." (See Und
Water definition below.)

Founders Stock

Shares in a company held by the initial founders, usually subject to cert
restrictions as to their disposition.

**Fully Diluted
Capitalization**

The total number of shares outstanding or set aside for issuance (such
shares in a stock option plan).

Going Public

See Initial Public Offering.

Immediate Vesting

When one company has been bought by another, all options that have
issued by the acquired company are automatically available for immedia
exercising, or vesting.

**Incentive Stock Options
(ISOs)**

ISOs can only be granted to employees, as opposed to outside consulta
or contractors. Their advantage is in allowing holders to acquire stock
without paying taxes on their gain in value until they sell the stock.

Incremental Vesting

Period of time during which options become vested gradually, such as
quarterly, which is specified in an option agreement. Such vesting is als
referred to as vesting on an incremental basis.

**Initial Public Offering
(IPO)**

An IPO is a company's first sale of stock to the public.

Insider

An insider is any officer, director, advisor, or investor of a company that
public or about to go public. Because of his or her inside knowledge of
company's financial plans, an insider is restricted in trading the compar
stock based on information not disclosed to the public.

Liquidity

How easily an investment holding can be converted into cash. Shares c
stock are liquid if there is a ready market for those shares, meaning tha
shares are available to be bought and sold. If a company is privately he
the stock is said to be illiquid.

Lockup Period

A period of time that insiders of a company are required by an underwr
hold onto shares of stock gained from exercising options before being
allowed to sell. Once individuals exercise options, they may not sell the
shares for the entire lockup period, often one year.

Long-term Capital Gains

Profits from an investment held longer than one year. These gains are
subject to tax rates that can be as high as 20%.

174

Nonqualified Stock Options (NSOs)	NSOs can be granted to anyone (employees, outside consultants, contractors, directors, and others). However, the recipient pays taxes on the difference between the price of the options and the value of the shares as soon as the shares are acquired, rather than when the shares are sold.
Offering Statement	A statement prepared by the underwriters and distributed to potential investors before a company goes public.
Option Agreement Letter	Document given by a company to an employee to legally grant options.
Option Grants	The number of shares a recipient can acquire via options.
Ordinary Income	Income subject to regular income tax rates, such as salary.
Par Value	The monetary value shown on a security.
Phantom Stock	Can be converted into real stock at some point in the future when certain predetermined events occur. Often referred to in the context of executive bonus plans tied to increases in a public company's share price.
Preferred Stock	A class of stock that has advantages over common stock in the event of sale or liquidation of the company.
Privately Held	A company that is owned by one or several individuals or institutions but not by the "public." Shares of privately-held companies are said to be illiquid.
Publicly Held	A company is considered publicly held—or owned by the public—if its shares are traded on a public stock exchange (like the New York Stock Exchange or NASDAQ). A company can be publicly held even if the majority of its shares are still owned by the company's original founders and investors.
Registration Statement	A statement required by the Securities and Exchange Commission in order for a company to conduct an IPO. This statement details all of the information that is relevant for the public to make informed judgments about the value of the company.
Repricing Options	When companies, usually publicly held, adjust the prices on stock options lower in consideration of a decline in their share prices, that puts employees "under water." Companies shy away from this practice because it means incurring an accounting charge against profits.
Restricted Stock	Stock available for purchase immediately upon joining a company, but

175

subject to vesting and other conditions.

Securities and Exchange Commission (SEC)	The federal agency charged with ensuring that the investing public has access to all of the relevant and material information about every public company traded on a US market.
Shares	Ownership in a company. Usually referred to as shares of stock.
Shares Authorized	The number of shares of stock that a company is allowed to issue, whet they are outstanding or are held in treasury by the company.
Shares Outstanding	Stock held by investors, as opposed to shares held in the company trea
Short-term Capital Gains	Profits from an investment held less than one year. These gains are su to taxes at regular income tax rates, which often exceed 20%.
Spread	When options are" "above water," the spread is the difference between grant price and the stock's market value.
Stock	Equity or ownership in a company commonly referred to as common sto
Stock Option Plan	An employee incentive plan that allows employees of a company the op to buy shares of stock in the company at a specified price at some poin the future.
Stock Options	These grant the right, but not the obligation, to buy shares of stock at a specified price within a particular time interval, and with a specific expir date.
Stock Purchase Plan	A plan to encourage employees to take a personal financial stake in the company by offering shares of stock for purchase at a discount—usuall the range of 10-15%— over their "open market" purchase price.
Stock Split	Companies will often declare a split, often a 2-for-1 split, which will redu by half the price per share and double the amount of shares outstandin
Strike Price	The price at which an option holder may buy shares of stock. Often refe to as the exercise price.
Under Water	If an option does not allow the purchase of shares of stock for less than market price of those shares, the option is said to be "under water."
Underwriters	Investment bankers who in effect buy a stake in the company and then

176

this stake to the public. The underwriter guarantees a minimum price for the sale of the company in return for a premium on the shares sold to the public if demand outstrips supply.

Venture Capital Firms   Investment vehicles funded by wealthy individuals looking to take risky stakes in promising new companies and technologies in return for both control and a share of future profits.

Vesting Period   Period of time during which the option holder is allowed to exercise incrementally more options that have already been granted. Vesting typically occurs over periods of three to five years in corresponding increments of 20% to 30% vested per year.

Warrants   An investment vehicle similar to options, allowing for purchase of stock at a specific price before a particular date or in the future.

Appendix C

Sample Offer Letter

High Tech Wizards Inc.
Main Street
Successville, USA

Alice Smith   January 1, 2000
100 Acorn Place
Anytown, USA

Dear Alice:

I am pleased to advise you that High Tech Wizards (the "Company") has awarded you an incentive stock option to purchase Fifteen Thousand (15,000) shares of the Common Stock, $.01 par value per share, of the Company at a price of $0.10 per share, for a total exercise price of $1,500. The Company is making this offer to certain key employees to "share the business" with valued employees and encourage them to stay with the Company. Hopefully, by owning a piece of the Company, you will continue your efforts at helping the Company grow and succeed. Regardless of your decision whether or not to buy, you are requested to keep the number of shares for which you are eligible strictly confidential.

The following terms and conditions are applicable with respect to this option, and your signature below shall constitute your acknowledgment and acceptance of same:

(a)   This option shall not be transferable under any circumstances. During your lifetime, this option is only exercisable by you.

(b)   The price at *which this* option may be exercised shall be $0.10 per share, for a total of $1,500.

(c)   This option is exercisable commencing March 1, 2000, and at any time thereafter prior to March 19, 2009, subject to the following terms:

   (1)   Should your employment terminate with the Company (or parent or subsidiary of the Company) for any reason other than death or disability as defined in Internal Revenue Code, Section 22(e)(3), as amended (the "Code"), all unexercised options shall terminate immediately.

   (2)   In the event of termination of your employment as a result of your death, the outstanding options exercisable by you at the date of your death may be exercised by your estate until one (1) year from the date of your death.

   (3)   In the event of termination of your employment as a result of your disability, as above defined, or in the event of a disability that lasts for more than ninety (90) days, all outstanding options exercisable by you at the date of such termination shall terminate three (3) months from the date.

(d)   Notwithstanding anything herein to the contrary, the maximum extent to which this option may be exercised is as follows:

Dates	UP-TO
January 1, 2000 to January 1, 2001	0%
January 1, 2001 to January 1, 2002	33%
January 1, 2002 to January 1, 2003	66%
January 1, 2003 to January 1, 2004	100%

(e)   This option may be exercised in whole or in part from time to time provided, however, that an option may not be exercised as to less

180

than one hundred (100) shares at any one time unless it is being exercised in full and the balance of shares subject to option is less than one hundred (100).

(f)   The shares of Common Stock underlying this option and the exercise price therefore shall be appropriately adjusted from time to time for stock splits, reverse splits, stock dividends and reclassifications of shares.

(g)   In the event of a sale or acquisition of substantially all of the stock or assets of the Company, the Company shall give at least thirty (30) days' notice of such an event to you and you may exercise up to 100% of this option; if you do not exercise the option within thirty (30) days of such notice, all unexercised portions of this option shall terminate and be of no further force or effect.

This opportunity to purchase stock in the Company is being offered because of the Company's desire to reward continuing loyal service. Exercising options may not be a prudent business decision for some employees. Therefore, we urge you to review this opportunity carefully and make a decision to exercise options only if your personal financial situation makes this a wise choice.

When you wish to exercise this stock option, please refer to the provisions of this letter and then correspond in writing with the Secretary of the Company. Further, please indicate your acknowledgment and acceptance of this option by signing the enclosed copy of this letter and returning it to the undersigned.

Very truly yours,

George Washington
President

ACKNOWLEDGEMENT ANDACCEPTANCE:

_____

Alice Smith

181

Appendix D

Index

185

9 780970 118127